WHEN THE HEART CRIES BUT NEVER BREAKS

A Novel Set in Vietnam 1975—1979

Duyen Nguyen

WHEN THE HEART CRIES BUT NEVER BREAKS

A NOVEL SET IN VIETNAM 1975—1979

DUYEN NGUYEN

PUBLISHED BY

A FICTION IMPRINT FROM ADDUCENT
ADDUCENT, INC.
WWW.ADDUCENT.CO

TITLES DISTRIBUTED IN
North America
United Kingdom
Western Europe
South America
Australia
China
India

When the Heart Cries but Never Breaks
A Novel Set in Vietnam 1975—1979
By Duyen Nguyen

© COPYRIGHT 2016 BY DUYEN NGUYEN—ALL RIGHTS RESERVED
BY THE U.S. COPYRIGHT ACT OF 1976, THE SCANNING, UPLOADING, AND ELECTRONIC SHARING OF ANY PART OF THIS BOOK WITHOUT THE PERMISSION OF THE AUTHOR AND/OR PUBLISHER CONSTITUTE UNLAWFUL PIRACY AND THEFT OF THE AUTHOR'S INTELLECTUAL PROPERTY. IF YOU WOULD LIKE TO USE MATERIAL FROM THE BOOK (OTHER THAN FOR REVIEW PURPOSES), PRIOR WRITTEN PERMISSION MUST BE OBTAINED BY CONTACTING THE AUTHOR OR PUBLISHER. THANK YOU FOR YOUR SUPPORT OF AUTHOR'S RIGHTS.

ISBN: 9781937592530 (PAPERBACK)

Library of Congress Catalog Number: 2016951911

PUBLISHED BY ADDUCENT, INC. UNDER ITS *ESCRIRE* FICTION IMPRINT
JACKSONVILLE, FLORIDA
WWW.ADDUCENT.CO
WWW.ADDUCENTINC.COM
PUBLISHED IN THE UNITED STATES OF AMERICA

This book is a work of fiction. Names, characters, places and incidents are the products of the author's imagination or are used fictitiously. Any resemblance to actual persons, living or dead is purely coincidental.

DEDICATION & ACKNOWLEDGMENTS

This novel is dedicated to those who were detained, tortured and murdered in the *re-education camps, new economy zones* and prisons under the Vietnamese Communist Regime.

I'd like to acknowledge the following former prisoners I interviewed for the book:

NGUYEN ANH TUAN
TANG VAN MUOI
TANG HUU HANH
NGUYEN MINH DUONG
PHAM VU

Nguyen Minh Duong

Pham Vu

"When the evacuation is ordered, the signal will be read on Armed Forces Radio. That signal is: *'The temperature in Saigon is 105 degrees and rising.'* This will be followed by the playing of, *I'm Dreaming of a White Christmas.*"

That announcement triggered *Operation Frequent Wind*, the almost unbelievable evacuation plan executed by United States forces on the 29th and 30th of April, 1975 when more than 7,000 people were evacuated by helicopter from various points in Saigon. The total number of Vietnamese evacuated or self-evacuated, ending up in the custody of the United States for processing as refugees to enter the country, totaled 138,869.

But hundreds of thousands were left behind that then faced 're-education' by the victors. The re-education camps, modeled on Soviet Gulags (and in some cases operated similarly as a Nazi concentration camp) soon became full. The New Economic Zone programs announced were thinly veiled justification for the confiscation of all assets held by the South Vietnamese people.

The smoke had cleared over Vietnam, but the country still ran with blood.

At least 150 re-education prisons were built after Saigon fell. One in three South Vietnamese families had a relative in a re-education camp. In such camps, the government imprisoned over one million former military officers, government workers, and supporters of the former government of South Vietnam. According to published academic studies in the United States and Europe, 165,000 people died in the camps. Thousands more that survived were tortured or abused. Many were imprisoned for as long as 17 years, with most terms ranging from three to 10 years.

All of the above was done by the Socialist Republic of Vietnam in an attempt at transforming *sinful or incomplete* individuals into obliging and loyal citizens of their new republic. In reality, it was both a means of revenge and as a sophisticated technique of repression and indoctrination.

Those who were imprisoned fell into two categories: 1) Those who were detained in re-education camps from 1975 because they collaborated with the other side during the war. And 2) Those who were arrested in the years after 1975 for attempting to exercise such democratic freedoms as those mentioned in Article 11 of the 1973 Paris Agreements. Both categories of prisoners were held in direct violation of Article 11 of the 1973 Paris Agreements, an international treaty, and therefore of international law. They were never tried, judged or convicted of any crime. Many South Vietnamese, mislead by the new regime, entered these camps in the hope of reconciliation and hoped to return to a country finally at peace. They dreamed they would be able to continue their lives without war and bloodshed. But instead, many lived years in a nightmare. An untold number died in the camps.

CHAPTER 1

They had moved him at night as they had half a dozen times. He had lost track of how much time had passed. His new dwelling was a metal container. Every camp he had been in had them, usually around the perimeter of the camp near the latrines and barbed wire fence. He knew from experience that being close to the fence didn't mean an easy escape even if he could get out. The occasional explosions of a prisoner trying to get away through the minefields that encircled the camps told him how deadly that supposed path to freedom could be.

No one other than guards, at any of the camps, had spoken to him. And they only spoke roughly in Vietnamese, which he knew only a little of, or crudely—mostly American GI curse words—in English. For a while, he had talked to himself, but even the appeal of doing that had faded, and he now remained silent.

At first, he tried to exercise and keep his strength, but he was fed so little that eventually, he lacked energy. Most of his time was spent in remembering what his life had once been. The largest, most detailed memory that played through his mind, especially at night, was both a nightmare and relief. The images from it would haunt him as long as he lived, which as he weakened and his spirit faded, probably would not be long. In that memory, he had been shot and had fallen. From the ground, he had seen his loved ones get on the last helicopter out of Saigon. The North Vietnamese Army and the Vietcong were flooding the area. They were the victors taking possession. He had seen him — the man he would always associate with losing the most important things in his world — standing over him with a twisted snarl on his face as he thrust it into his. Far behind him, over the man's shoulder, he had seen the helicopter climbing away through the smoke-filled sky over Saigon. The man followed his look and turned back to kick him where the machine gun had torn open his side. "You'll never see them again!"

The pain that spasmed through him closed his eyes. He knew that at best he was going to be killed but at worst feared they would imprison and torture him as they had before. But those thoughts couldn't prevent him from opening them as he struggled to his knees to take one last look at the now small dark speck on the horizon headed south and toward the sea. Fleeing to the safety of U.S. Navy ships they had heard were waiting to take aboard what evacuees they could hold. He sank back to the ground. The man looked down at him then bent to press a pistol to his head; its barrel centered on his forehead just above the bridge of his nose and between his eyes. He turned his head away, and the man repositioned the gun to put its muzzle in his ear. What was going to happen to him didn't matter. He closed his eyes again, thankful that they had escaped.

* * *

SUMMER 1978
SUOI MAU RE-EDUCATION CAMP
NEAR BIEN HOA

"He is there?" the voice was level, steady with just a hint of line static to show the call was from some distance away.

Quan, the camp commander, recognized the voice though he had spoken with the man only once before when he had told him to expect a prisoner who would not be identified in any paperwork. Afterward, he had checked the man out and had been told by his contacts that he was someone it was best to listen to carefully. And a voice to obey given the growing reputation of the ruthless man behind it. "Yes. He arrived at..." he referred to the notes on his desk, "at 02:12 am." Quan was still stunned at what he had discovered when the man was removed from the box he had traveled in secured in the back of the transport truck. But he knew better than to comment on or even mention it.

"Was there any trouble with him?"

"None that the drivers reported." Seeing the prisoner's condition, Quan didn't see how he could conceivably have caused any. "He was quiet, kept his head down, and is now in a solid wall container cell."

"Away from all other prisoners in your camp?"

"Yes. As you instructed in your call the other day regarding him." Quan knew what the man—this new prisoner—was but not who. He didn't want to know anything more about him. "He's away from the camp's barracks and in an area with restricted access." He was troubled by now being part of something that could have significant risk to him not just professionally but also personally. It was too late now, though. The man was here in his camp.

"Good... good..." The line went dead.

CHAPTER 2

SUOI MAU RE-EDUCATION CAMP

Tuan Anh Nguyen knew that they moved prisoners from camp to camp to prevent them from making friends and hatching escape plans. The moves also made it more difficult for outside groups to help prisoners escape. That's why the long-term, called re-education but really concentration, camps looked more like prison compounds than schools. He had been moved four times over three and a half years.

    They weren't far from Bien Hoa and the railroad station in the Tan Hiep District. This camp he was now in was one he knew having been here before. He had landed here with the 300 81st Airborne Rangers when they were airlifted by Chinook helicopters to this, then new, base camp. He had been part of a newly formed special unit, the Tactical Operations Headquarters, commanded by Lieut. Col. Vu Tuan Thong. That was in January 1975. It was only months later when it had fallen, overrun by the North Vietnamese Army making full-scale assaults at all bases on their path to Saigon.

This time, he had arrived at Suoi Mau in the back of a truck. The last in a convoy of eight, with dozens of other men who looked as exhausted and underfed as he did. As he got out of the truck, covered in dust from the billows of dirt, he scanned the area. The camp was divided into five sub-camps, numbered from K-1 to K-5, all encircled by eight-feet high barbed wire fences. Beyond the outer barrier, which was dotted with telephone line poles with lights mounted on them, he could see the cleared area that told him there was a minefield that extended 30 or 40 feet beyond the perimeter of the camp. Seeing the armed guards in the towers at each corner of the sub-camps, he shook his head. He thought of his love of history and how, when he had read about the Holocaust during World War II, he had wondered how prisoners at Dachau, Auschwitz and others equally associated with the evils and depravity of men, managed to survive. He knew that somehow, someway, he was going to find out firsthand. If the hard labor didn't kill him.

In his past camps, he had worked in a quarry, in the jungle clearing bamboo for expansion and in the fields six days a week for ten hours a day. He and his fellow prisoners were always thirsty and always hungry. There was never enough to drink and eat. The Communists wanted them to be weak and easily controlled. This was their re-education, he spat on the ground.

The processing was the same at each camp; rudimentary, but meticulous in its sameness. They confirmed his name, his previous rank in the South Vietnamese Army and previous camps he had been in and for how long. The young woman in front of him from the cadre wasn't ugly but also didn't have the looks and appearance that male senior officers and staff commanders seemed to covet. She likely would rise no further than her present rank. He wondered how that felt to her, after all, she was one of the victors, too. He knew that her own comrades would hold her back; even where everyone was supposed to share and benefit equally, someone had to do the jobs no one wanted to do.

He smiled at her as she checked off the paperwork and assigned him to one of the barracks. When she saw his smile, she dropped her eyes and looked away for a moment and then almost shyly spoke with him.

"You are in barracks number three." She pointed at its location on a map that she now held in her hand showing the layout of the camp. Thankful for an eidetic memory, he fixed its position and that of the other structures within the camp in his mind. He blinked for a moment to freeze it in mind and then saw that she had flipped the page on her clipboard from the map to a list of what appeared to be work assignments. "You look strong." Her eyes shifted away again for a moment and then came back to him. "Gathering construction and raw materials... it is hard work but necessary for our country."

Tuan saw her eyes sweep over him. He knew he was handsome, without being arrogant about it, and that he was in better shape than most men. His looks were also enhanced by the fact that most of the group he had come in with were older. Many of them had their heads down as they were processed—some seemed ashamed and would not make eye contact. Tuan couldn't do that. They had been defeated. Yes. But beaten? No. The Communists couldn't take his pride. They couldn't kill the love he still held for his country that he and so many fallen friends had fought so desperately for. He lifted his eyes and met her gaze.

CHAPTER 3

SUOI MAU RE-EDUCATION CAMP

Chau watched the young man she had processed the day before. His record showed that he had been moved from several camps over the last three years, but he looked remarkably healthy and far younger than most of the men. She too had moved from camp to camp and wondered if she would find a spot somewhere in the cadre where she would be appreciated and could rise in rank. The new Vietnam was supposed to be about equal opportunity but as a loyal cadre member, she had not seen it yet and was beginning to question what that really meant for her. She worked as hard as the men and always seemed to draw some of the toughest duties. She walked into the storage building and stockyard for materials and was soon sweating as much as the men pushing wheelbarrows full of stone to be weighed and stockpiled for trucks to pick up later to take to construction sites.

She looked again at the tall young man and smiled. Straightening to wipe his forehead with his hand, he glanced at her and caught the expression on her face for a moment before she turned and walked away.

*　*　*

A Week Later

Tuan had seen them at other camps, and Suoi Mau was no different. There were a half a dozen metal Conex containers located in different areas around the camp's perimeter. They were industrial shipping containers that the Communists used as holding cells or as punishment for prisoners that were not responding to re-education. They felt that a period of solitary confinement in a metal container with just a few holes to let air in would serve as a means to change their thinking; to make them conform to the new order of things in Vietnam.

There was one next to the concrete block building where they delivered the wood and stone, construction materials, they gathered each day. When he had first arrived, it had been empty like all the others as evidenced by its open doors. But now those doors were closed—thickly barred shut top and bottom—and some newly added ventilation holes had been cut through its metal walls. A small, shoebox size, opening had also been cut out near the bottom of the door. He knew what that was for... it was how the prisoner inside got their food and water. Assuming they were allowed any.

As he worked, usually toward the end of the work day, he occasionally saw the young woman, the cadre officer who had processed him, he had met that first morning in camp. He had learned her name was Chau, and her main duties were to check in, receive and then check out and distribute the materials stored in the concrete block building. One afternoon, she stood nearby with her clipboard and was writing something down, but he saw her eyes dart up to watch him as he unloaded wheelbarrows of stone. He wiped his face and shoulders with a piece of canvas he'd found and kept as a kerchief. As he moved the now empty wheelbarrows out of the building to where other prisoners could pick them up to reload, she followed him. He turned and smiled at her.

"Hello again."

Maybe it was because they were at one end of the Yard and halfway between the prisoner's barracks and the cadre's huts and the commander's office and that the buildings were angled away from them that she looked at him and smiled back.

"Hello." It seemed like she might not say anything else but then she added, "I knew you were strong and could do the work." Her admiring gaze traveled over his arms and chest to look into his eyes.

He looked away from her to scan the area, and his eyes lingered on the Conex container nearby. It too was set equidistant from the prisoners and cadre quarters. He could see the spill of dust and what might be a piece of tattered shirt or pants behind the opening in the door. Whoever was inside was no doubt trying to press as close as possible to the only opening of any size that would let in any bit of wind or fresh air.

Facing her again he returned her look, still smiling, and let his eyes drop to her breasts and then back up to her eyes. That shyness flashed in them. "Yes, but I don't know for how long. Even though I'm young and healthy if you've been around these camps for very long, as I have, then you know eventually that changes." He didn't smile as he said that and instead let the full sadness he felt come through. She looked uncomfortable but still met his gaze as he studied her.

* * *

The man was of average height but at one time must've been overweight. Tuan could tell by how the belt had holes notched in it to draw his pants tight. Or perhaps they were pants donated to him or that he found, and he had taken what he could get. He seemed familiar to him and thought he might share the same barracks with him. He watched as the man stopped and stacked his load of stone; the same task he was doing. Slowing to time their finish together Tuan straightened and turned. He caught the young woman, Chau, watching them and smiled at her. Her eyes flicked at the other man and then came back to him. As they passed her to exit the material yard, he knew better than to turn to the man at his side. It was never wise to let any cadre guard know you were friendly with any particular person in the camps. He looked straight ahead and spoke softly. "My name is Tuan. I think we share a barracks... I believe I saw you talk to my friend Van."

The man nodded. "I saw you talking with him, too. He's a good man." His voice was low and deeper than Tuan's, but clear. "He doesn't talk much, but I see how he acts and that he always helps others."

They both quieted as two cadre guards approached them heading in the opposite direction watching closely, without making eye contact, until they passed and were safely a dozen yards behind them.

"He fixes things around the camp, and he knows much." He coughed and continued. "My name is Phu..." He paused coughing again. "You must be, too. Be a good man that is if Van is your friend. I don't think he is the type to make just anyone a friend."

"He has always been like that—an honorable man." Tuan paused to think about what he should share. "We served together—fought together."

Phu darted a glance up at Tuan, who was a few inches taller. "Now here you are... with him again."

Out of the corner of his eye, Tuan saw the flash of a smile on his face. He couldn't tell what Phu meant by his statement or if it had another intent. But it was accurate. He nodded once and felt the tightness in his jaw. "Yes, here we are."

They entered the barracks and separated. Phu stopped near the front at his cot. He raised a hand, palm out, and nodded at Tuan, who acknowledged with the same gesture then headed to the back of the barracks.

CHAPTER 4

Chau's Quarters
Suoi Mau Re-Education Camp

The two girls she shared quarters with were often out late and sometimes not back until early morning. She assumed they were with men from the commander's staff. Maybe even the commander himself. She knew that many of them—the men—brought women, administration, and clerks mostly, into their private quarters at night.

Chau's roommates barely acknowledged her existence. So she sat alone in their room. Her side was decidedly more Spartan than theirs. The bed was regulation with its thin blanket and almost equally thin pillow that she folded in half to provide some comfort and support to her neck and head as she slept. Her only personal item was a hand mirror with the small flowers that she had painted on it and given as a gift years ago to her mother who had died during the Hanoi bombings. It was the only thing in her possessions she had asked her father for. He had died not long after that.

She had affixed a wire loop from the handle and the mirror now hung from a hook on the wall next to her bed. She hadn't held it since hanging it there months ago when she had reported to this camp, to Suoi Mau. She lifted it from the hook. For the 1000th time, she wished her mom had not gone to Hanoi to visit her cousin. Up until her death in the U.S. bombing raids, Chau had quietly envied Americans. She especially liked their movies and music. She really did not understand why Americans were aiding the South but didn't consider them enemies. That was until she saw her mother's body. But she had also seen her own countrymen—North Vietnamese—do terrible things to South Vietnamese and American prisoners of war. Just in this camp, she had seen the abuse, the beatings, and torture. The withholding of food and water to keep— they were not supposed to refer to them as prisoners— the men here weak and easier to re-educate.

It had struck her as odd, when she thought of her life here in camp, that it was one of the imprisoned men that was nicest to her. She knew the likely reason, but he seemed genuine... the look in his unusual, slate-gray, eyes was sincere. Despite that, she knew she was playing with fire. If she were caught paying attention or even worse favoring one of the prisoners, the punishment would be severe. She looked around and wondered if where she would be sent, as a consequence, could be worse than this. Was this to be her life—shared quarters in a squalid camp—for years to come? Couldn't she steal something, have someone. For her own enjoyment. She relaxed her arms that had been tightly wrapped around her knees pulling them to her chest. A deep breath she hadn't realized she had been holding released as she ran one hand up the smoothness of her thigh and wished it was his hand.

* * *

MATERIAL WAREHOUSE
SUOI MAU RE-EDUCATION CAMP

Tuan had seen her watching him and could tell by the tone of her voice that she liked him. When he told her, he didn't know how long he could go on and actually survive from camp to camp and the hard, unrelenting, labor he had not been joking. It all was slowly grinding him down. This was the only time, in any of the camps, that someone had seemed to show a shred of understanding and kindness toward him. He needed to leverage that and do whatever he could either to make his life easier or set up the conditions for some way that he could escape.

"Maybe things will become better for you."

He knew she wanted to sound as if she was reassuring him but he could tell she had her own doubts. He pointed at the metal prison cell not far from them. "Will things get better for whoever is inside there, too?"

"That prisoner is not my concern." She looked up at him.

"Are there any prisoners that do concern you?"

She didn't immediately respond and kept making notes in the ledger she held as he moved bags of concrete mix for her to count. She thought about this young man that she had met under the most unfortunate of circumstances for them both. And then she thought about herself. Chau's ill-fitting uniform hid her sturdy body with its voluptuous curves. Since leaving her town, near Lạng Sơn, in northern Vietnam close to the Chinese border and joining the military she had never received any clothing that flattered her figure. She had tried to alter the first uniform she had been issued to fit her better, but when her superior officer found her doing so, she had been cruelly reprimanded: "The state has given you what to wear—you do not make changes to it." So she wore what they gave her, and it bunched too tight in places and was too loose in others. The overall result was that her plain features, which were only what most saw, were not that appealing and men did not pay too much attention to her. Tuan startled her by touching her arm. Her eyes shifted away from him, but her body didn't move; his left hand remained on her arm. She tingled at the touch. The electric charge intensified when she looked up and saw him studying her. "There is one..." she slowly, almost shyly, moved a step closer to him. "That I think I could care for." She closed her eyes and turned her face up to his.

He took a deep breath. He knew that once he started down this path, it would be not just dangerous; playing on emotions was treacherous and not something he did easily. But it was his only chance. He bent and kissed her lightly on the lips both hands now stroking her shoulders and reaching around to draw her closer to him.

Her hand reached up and touched his face, a trembling finger tracing his jaw line to his chin. She was still close to him... near enough for the rise and fall of her breasts to brush his chest. "I think there's a way, for both of us, to make things better."

She knew she shouldn't speak so much to him, but he was nice to her. Chau wasn't naïve. She knew that it was likely he was trying to make a friend that could help him. At some point, he'd ask her for a favor but so far he had not.

"You're strong, Tuan." She watched as he bent back to his work and shifted the bag of concrete mix to get a grip on it then lifted to add it to those that had already been counted. She straightened, pressing both hands to the small of her back as she stretched. It was hot inside the concrete block building, and she had unbuttoned her tunic. Her undershirt was soaked with sweat and conformed to the arc of her high, firm, breasts. As she leaned forward, it pulled down enough to show the cleft of her cleavage. She saw his eyes flicker—a quick glance at it—then to her face. He seemed embarrassed, and she liked that. In her small town, boys had never paid any attention to her and since joining the service her only encounter with a fellow, male, cadre had started with him leering at her chest and grabbing at her. It ended as she kicked him away from her.

"You are, too." Tuan wiped his mouth with the back of his hand. Noticing it, she gave him her canteen. He took two swallows and spun the cap back on and returned it to her. He knew something was up—something had changed — when she told him that morning: "Tuan, you will help me with inventory today." He had nodded without comment but darted a warning at Phu, who had traces of a grin curving his lips.

He followed as she moved toward the front of the building and its entrance. Standing just inside she opened her tunic, fanning it at her sides, to let air circulate. The breeze coming in, even with its stench of the open latrines, felt good. He thought again of whoever it was locked in the metal container not far from them.

"And you seem dependable." She looked over her shoulder at him.

Tuan realized she was continuing with what she had said minutes ago. He had turned away when she loosened her tunic then changed his mind and watched as she buttoned her tunic and straightened her uniform. Suddenly she was very businesslike, and the tone was clearly of someone in authority speaking to someone they expected to follow orders. She now had her notepad out and was writing something in it.

"I think since you seem so responsible and trustworthy that, on some days, I will assign you to sort out the daily rations and deliver them to the camp." With the last stab of her pen on the paper, she flipped the pad closed and looked at him. Her face did not show any emotion but there was something in the depth of her eyes—in the look she gave him.

"I will not let you down, Chau." His voice was just as even toned and formal as hers had been. But he knew this was a dramatic change in their relationship. He wondered where it might lead.

CHAPTER 5

THE YARD
SUOI MAU RE-EDUCATION CAMP

"That young, female, cadre guard..." Phu's voice was flat and noncommittal, "she watches you. She must think you are real trouble." He scanned the open expanse of ground, a cleared area between the main buildings of the camp, the guard and prisoner quarters and the storage warehouse. Used for a staging area for working parties, trucks to transport them and for material loading, right now it was clear of guards.

Tuan shrugged his shoulders, his hands not leaving the wheelbarrow as he pushed it along parallel with Phu's. They approached the flatbed truck that would take them to the crude stone quarry that was their work assignment for the week.

"Maybe she thinks you will suddenly turn into a movie hero." Phu teased. "Like that American actor, the tall one who squints, Clint Eastwood and will break out or free us all!"

"You're amusing, Phu." Tuan worried that the guards would see them and think there was too much talking going on even though they kept working. Concern about that perception was always there when he was around Phu, but he had grown to like him a lot and enjoyed his company. "I don't think so."

"Maybe..." Phu paused and did his own examination, of who might be nearby as they stopped beside the truck. Tuan helped him lift his wheelbarrow onto the truck bed as one of the other prisoners pulled it forward and turned it wheels up beside the other equipment. A line of men behind Tuan and Phu brought up their work tools for loading. Soon the back of the truck was full of wheelbarrows, picks, and shovels.

Just as they finished, two guards approached carrying six canteens for the 12-man work crew. Tuan and Phu would share one, and it was all they would have to drink for their 10-hour workday. One of the guards, Tuan knew he was the driver from the day before, jerked a thumbs-up gesture that meant for the crew to get on the truck. Most of them had to sit on the equipment. Tuan and Phu managed to get the best spot at the end of the truck bed where they sat with their legs dangling off the back.

The truck moved out and soon a cloud of dirt dust was billowing around them. Rolling along, the movement left it behind to spread across the windshield of the dump truck behind them.

"So..." Phu's voice was louder. "About that young woman."

Tuan knew they could not be heard but if the truck behind them got close enough, the driver would see them and would then report how long they had talked. He wiped grit and sand from his eyes as he turned his face toward Phu. In that quick look, he saw the curve of the grin on his face.

"So..." Phu continued. "Maybe this young lady, perhaps she's not just vigilant—a good communist cadre. Maybe she likes you?"

Tuan knew that Phu had seen a few of Chau's unguarded looks and was already convinced that might be the case. But he couldn't agree with or confirm it—her interest in him—with Phu. What was going on with her might be to his benefit, but it was also very dangerous. "I think you see things, Phu." Tuan hoped he would leave it at that.

Phu sensed his new, young, friend's discomfort and laughed, which brought in a mouthful of dust and dirt that made him cough. He spat it out as the truck slowed to make a turn. Checking to make sure the dump truck behind them had not closed the distance he continued. "I think she sees things... I believe that what she sees is my good looking friend!" He slapped

Tuan on the shoulder but then cut his teasing short as the truck slowed more and then stopped.

"Get out and unload!" The driver shouted at the men still on the truck. Tuan was off first and then steadied Phu as he dropped to the ground. They looked at each other. Phu no longer smiled. He looked down at his blistered hands—they never seemed to toughen—and sighed. The sound was soul-deep and full of ache. He reached up, with Tuan, to grip and then lower their two wheelbarrows. He studied his friend's young face, just now showing the lines of a maturing man. He hoped that young woman could make things easier for him. Though he hoped for the best for them all, he had no illusions. His propensity for observing the machinations of those around him and then talking—speaking out—about them was what got him on a watch and reward list, and that was what had brought the Communists down on him. He looked at his hands again, wincing as he gripped the wooden handles of the barrow, and prayed that this woman's attention remained unnoticed by others and did not result in his friend's death.

CHAPTER 6

Mid-summer
Suoi Mau Re-Education Camp

He had convinced Chau to let him not only deliver the food at sundown when all the work parties were back in but also to carry the food to the prisoner in the metal container. "Who is the person in there?" He pointed at the metal container everyone knew was really a prison cell, Tuan felt comfortable enough with Chau, now to ask her that. "It's the only one in the whole camp that's occupied."

Chau stroked his arm. They were inside the doorway of the storage building and out of sight. "No one important." She did not even look in the direction of the container.

"It doesn't matter if they are someone important. In this heat, it is stifling inside, and they must be suffering. Isn't there any way to help... can I give them extra water?"

"No." She let go of his arm and looked up at him. "Just push his food and water in and leave. Don't get caught hanging around."

"So it's some man." Tuan touched her shoulder, and he could feel her slight tremble. She was so easily aroused. "Who is it?"

She shrugged and moved closer to embrace him. "I don't know. No one does other than Quan, the camp commander."

"Do you see him as just a prisoner; another unknown and unnamed person—not a human being—imprisoned." Tuan wanted to remove her arms from him but knew she would take that as a slight. But he wanted her to understand how he felt.

"The government does not consider this a prison," Chau remarked trying to defend what she had grown up being taught to protect.

Tuan shook his head. "Look around you, Chau." He pulled at the worn shirt he wore with its rips and crudely stitched repairs he had made using smuggled in needle and thread. He slapped his hand against his side, striking the prominently displayed ribs through the torn cloth. "Look at me… and the other men. Most of us are starving to death but slowly." He took her hand trying to get her to face him.

She wouldn't, and with her head down replied. "These—this camp—are places where men and women are rehabilitated through education and socially productive labor."

"It sounds like they taught you to say that. Maybe to tell yourself that what you see being done every day to human beings is justified. But it's not." He let go of her hand. "When I was at a camp up north… the first one I was sent to… despite the harshness of the war the northerners, the villagers never hated us or were cruel to prisoners working in the fields. I remember a woman who brought 5-gallon cans of water to us. She cried when she saw that we worked so hard. She seemed like good people. One day she brought me a Communist-issued shirt that wasn't branded." He tugged again at his tattered shirt. "This is what's left of it and if not for her I wouldn't have it. You're from the north, and I see that, inside, you are not like the other cadre… the other guards." She still would not look up at him. "Each camp I was sent to was further south. And in each one, the guards and commanders, all from the north, were more brutal." He paused to see if she would comment. She did not and he continued, "Did they—do they—act that way because there is no one around who knows them. No one they know that is watching to see what they do, to judge them?"

* * *

Delivering the daily food rations had become a dull routine but still much better than the hard labor working parties. Each time he had dropped off the daily rations for that solitary prisoner, he had greeted them with, "Here is your food and water. Eat, drink and stay strong." He had never received a reply.

That evening he had started to turn away from the large metal box and was not really looking forward to meeting Chau, who had become a grasping and cloying lover. But he was thankful for the reprieve from the tough daily labor. He heard movement inside the container and as he watched, a grimy hand pulled the bag of rice, the sweet potato and the plastic jug of water inside. A voice that sounded raspy with disuse asked him, "Do you speak English?"

Tuan was too shocked to reply at first to the apparently American voice. He had heard rumors that some of the camps had held American prisoners after the war, but he hadn't believed them. Even when his barracks mate Phu had told him that he had seen at least a dozen of them, wearing tattered and faded shreds of their uniforms, at a northern camp he had been in before Suoi Mau, he had not believed him. But that voice, coming from the Conex container, was of an American man. Tuan spoke fluent English and had worked daily with the U.S. Army. He could not be mistaken. "Yes," He told the man.

"What year is it?" a hoarse, muffled, voice asked.

"1978..." Tuan blinked and wondered how long the man had been held prisoner.

"Where am I, what camp and where?" The voice was louder and came from the opening near the bottom of the door.

Tuan knelt and bent closer to it. "Suoi Mau, Bloody Stream, just northeast of Bien Hoa." He straightened and scanned the area in the twilight. It was even darker in the shadows in front of the container, but he was late in meeting Chau and was worried she might come looking for him. Getting caught by her talking with the prisoner in solitary confinement would ruin his arrangement with her. Getting caught, talking with a secret American prisoner, by any of the other guards might get him shot. He bent again closer to the door opening. "I must go for now, but we will talk tomorrow evening." He stood and the voice stopped him.

"Wait... what's your name?"

"Tuan." he quickly checked the area for any movement.

"My name is Scott... Scott Reynolds."

Tuan hurried away, the name teasing and taunting his memory. Hadn't there been an American reporter by that name?

CHAPTER 7

Barracks 3
Suoi Mau Re-Education Camp

"What's wrong Tuan?" Phu asked. "It's almost lights out. You know you don't want to be caught outside then." They both had seen the consequences of that.

Tuan's cot in the back corner was against the wall and gave him at least some small element of privacy. But his new friend would always follow him to sit on the bunk next to his, or stand, and talk. Phu was one of the most talkative people he had ever met. He had opinions and comments about anything and everything going on in camp… and a lot of thoughts he was happy to share about such as what was going on in the great big world beyond the borders of Vietnam. Tuan shook his head at Phu. Now was not the time to chat with him but he felt he had to ask. "Nothing's wrong; I was just taking care of something."

"Something or someone?" Phu took great joy in teasing Tuan about Chau. "I wish I had something… or someone to take care of..." he smiled at Tuan who ignored what he had just said.

"Didn't you mention that once in the north at the camp you were in before coming here... that you had seen American soldiers still prisoners?"

"Yes." Phu looked puzzled. Tuan had scoffed at him when he had told him that. "Why do you ask?"

Tuan took out the piece of blanket he used as a washcloth and wiped his face and shook his head. "No reason... I was just curious if you still believed that was what you had seen."

Phu had a steady look as he nodded his head. "I know I did, and I think there are a lot of things that are still going on in our country..." he lowered his voice, "what used to be our country. That would surprise the world." He looked at Tuan with questioning eyes, but he was still silent, occupied with his own thoughts when, a couple of minutes later, the lights went out.

Tuan lay back and for the thousandth time recalled his last moment of freedom... and that he had used it to report to those who now kept him imprisoned:

He had been hiding in a friend's apartment, trying to figure what to do next when he got the announcement about the requirement to enter the re-education process. He knew he had to be on some list so thought it best to go ahead and get this rehabilitation business over with so he could get a fresh start in the new Vietnam. The morning he was to report, he had packed his belongings, all he owned went into a small bag. Other than what he wore he had two khaki uniform shirts and two pairs of pants. He hadn't any food stockpiled but had some money—he had thought he could use it to buy meals for a month. He had found an old abandoned bicycle with a broken chain and had managed to fix it. That morning he rode it to his designated area. When he arrived, he had been told that he and the others gathering there would be picked up for transportation to their re-education center. The gathering point was an old park. It's formerly grass covered ground had been churned to raw dirt and mud by communist tanks when they had rolled into Saigon. One of the green metal monsters sat nearby next to the three trees it had knocked down. From it flew their flag... a gold star on a red background. It shifted in the slight breeze and caught some morning sunlight. To him it looked like a puddle of blood... his countries blood. When he got there he had been greeted with another announcement from a communist cadre with a bullhorn standing on the tank and looking down at the gathering of men:

"While in transit, and upon your arrival, you must present yourselves with genuine remorse for your past actions and transgressions. Continue to do so as you undergo political re-education so you may return to society and participate in it properly. The process is conducted in a classroom setting, and the lessons will last up to 30 days, depending on your rank and position in the former South Vietnam."

He had leaned his bike against the tree and looked at the men around him and could see on their face everything from anger to hate, to resignation on two or three of them... but he had not seen any shame. He remembered he had wondered at what others saw on his face. Soon after the announcement, the trucks rolled up, and he and several other men loaded in the back. Several hours later, and far to the north, just before dawn he was at his first camp. It was there that he saw his first fellow prisoner beaten to death by the guards for violating one of the camp regulations. He had just gotten off the truck when it happened. He had learned, through their cursing at the prisoner, that the man had been a major, a Marine, and would not write a confession. The guards had taunted him until he hit one of them. The one he had struck kicked him away and as the four others pinned the man's arms and legs down. The guard used the butt of his rifle to repeatedly smash the man in the face. He kept doing it even when the man stopped breathing.

One of the cadres who was carrying a clipboard had then approached us. "Come with me." We followed him into the nearby long, narrow, rickety building that easily held the twenty or so of us. "Sit." We faced him. "Your re-education will include the discovery of the exploitation by 'American imperialism' of workers in other countries, and how the victory of Vietnam, led by the Communist Party, over the United States of America was inevitable. You will learn the glory of labor—how it gives you purpose in the Socialist Republic of Vietnam, and the generosity of the new government toward the rebels—those who fought for and with the Americans." The man had then tucked the clipboard under his arm and slowly walked to the door. His boot heels were loud on the wooden planking of the floor and then it was suddenly quiet as he reached it. Just outside the door, we could see the dead man on the ground.

    The cadre leader shook his head and at first, he had thought perhaps the senior guard was looking at the body and regretted what had happened. Then still standing in the doorway, the guard leader had turned, and his smile told me that thought was very wrong. "You will all write a confession of what you have done to resist the reunification efforts of the SVR. It does not matter how small; you must have committed some such transgressions... if you taught in a school, you inevitably mislead your students to preserve the evil regime in the south... if you delivered mail, you were part of the United States puppet-war machinery. If you were a priest, you are guilty of providing spiritual comfort to those who fought against those that only wanted what was best for Vietnam. Or perhaps you are guilty of even more significant crimes..." he had then looked over his shoulder, out the door, meaningfully and then back at us as he continued, "such as being a soldier." He had then slapped the clipboard against his thigh and strode back in front of us. "You will all write your confessions." His smile had grown larger while his eyes sharpened and coldly glinted.

Haunted by that memory, it was hours later before Tuan was finally able to fall asleep.

* * *

When he woke, Tuan realized that he had continued to dream of that first morning at his first re-education camp:

He had left the classroom and was sure he would see it again as he had similar ones in the other camps he had been held in. The cadre charade of lecturing about the new Vietnam's policies and how they presented great opportunities would go on seemingly forever. But at least, if he was in there he wasn't sweating while chopping down and clearing bamboo or some other equally exhausting or dangerous job.

That first morning the instructor's last command had been, "locate your barracks... drop what you're carrying now there." He had looked at the bags, large and small at the feet of the men ranged in rows of desks before him. The owners of the small bags all looked like they had come from other camps; with each one they had carried with them less and less. Those with larger bags were likely fresh caught first-timers. Their wide-eyed looks also identified them as new to the re-education process. The instructor was still talking. "And muster back here in 30 minutes." Most of the men no longer had watches, but that didn't seem to matter. It was understood that they all needed to have a well-honed sense of urgency and concern about timeliness when obeying camp rules and the instructions from those now in charge of their lives.

He had stood and moved out with the others. The sun was bright, and one ray slanted down and was squarely in the pool of blood just outside the classroom door turning it a dark ruby color. It and some teeth and shards of bone within the congealing blood were all that remained of the body. Intuitively knowing not to stare too long at it—guards watched for that sort of behavior—he had oriented himself and headed where he thought his barracks should be.

His mind shifted back to a more recent memory, his first morning at this camp. Chau, who had processed him into the camp, had told him to find his barracks, leave any personal belongings and then report back to the classroom for his first indoctrination lecture by the camp commander. The expanse of hard-packed dirt — the yard that was at the center of the camp—was bigger than he had thought based on the map of the camp he had seen briefly, so he walked faster. Being late was not tolerated, and that got you the type of attention you did not want. He had passed twelve poles, each with about six feet showing above the ground, driven into the sunbaked earth. He hadn't slowed, but he noted that several were discolored with blood and as he passed those that were closest to him he could smell the familiar stench of feces and urine from frequent use. It had told him a lot about this camp's commander. He would have to be extra careful. Twice before, in other camps, he had been staked out for one to three days as punishment. The second time—the longest—included a midnight beating. The sudden pain of the first lash had lifted him from his sunburned heat exhaustion and unconsciousness and then, after the 20th, it drove him back into it. The next morning, they cut him loose and left him to crawl back to his barracks. He had still been expected to be on time for his working party. He shook off the feeling that memory brought back. Ahead of him was what should be his assigned barracks. A man had been repairing a portion of the roof that sagged just a few feet from the only door that he saw into the building.

"Excuse me." He had stopped at the door and looked up at the man who was three-quarters of the way up the ladder. "Is this barracks number three?"

The man had not looked down but answered. "Yes."

"Thank you." Inside had been rows of wooden frame bunks that ran the length of the building and were barely two feet apart. It was just like the last two camps. He had known he wouldn't be able to claim a bed until all the labor crews and working parties and camp workers were inside for the night. Sometimes that had been easy but twice before there had been difficulties. For some in the camps that small area was all they had, and they were fiercely possessive of their bunks. He had turned and gone out the door just as the man working on the roof was coming down the ladder. From a foot away they had recognized each other though it had been three years—nearly four—since he and Van had served together in the Quang Tri province. They both had noticed, at the same time, that a guard was approaching the barracks. Tuan knew better than to appear he had recognized his friend. Who with just a flash of acknowledgment, had been silent as well and quickly, without seeming to hurry, moved away with the ladder now under his arm. He had nodded at the guard as he passed him and then quick-marched to make it back to the classroom in time. He had hoped that Van was in Barracks 3, too and that he would get to talk to him that evening.

CHAPTER 8

Late Summer 1978
New Economic Zone
Near Long Khanh

Lan Uyen Tran had never been alone. Even when the Communists had taken their home, her mother had managed to keep the family together except for her father. He had been a colonel in the South Vietnamese Army and one of the first moved to a re-education camp. That was three years ago, and they hadn't seen him since. Then they had separated her from her mother and taken her to a new zone.

The camp where she was now located was headquarters for that particular zone. When she arrived, she discovered that part of her duties would be to provide housekeeping and cleaning services for the commander of the region, the man who had taken her from her mother. The camp was built on a hill with the commander's house at the top, and the other housing and buildings arranged lower toward the base. At the foot of the hill was a broad, clear, stream of water that supplied the camp. That was where the kitchen was located, and she made a three times a day seven days a week climb to bring meals to the commander. Remembering his hands on her once before she shuddered every time she was near him.

When the other girls and young women talked to her, some teased about how pretty she was but in the teasing was a mix of jealousy. And in some of them, it was a subtle warning tinged with worry and fear not just for her but about something they had experienced themselves that they were afraid to speak of.

"The commander has taken a liking to our young one here. I think he watches the clock for when she comes up the hill." The woman, Kim, was only a couple of years older than Lan. She was one of the females that seemed most jealous and harshest toward her at times.

"I don't know what you mean. I'm just here to do my work." Lan did not like to talk to her.

An older woman who'd been kind to Lan commented, "pay no attention to her—she's just upset because the commander no longer looks at her."

Lan had tried to ignore Kim and wished the commander's interest had remained on her. At night, her dreams were filled with nightmares of what would happen if he was ever alone with her.

CHAPTER 9

Early Fall 1978
The Conex Container
Suoi Mau Re-Education Camp

"If Bach is still watching me, and I'm sure he is, he's going to move me at some point, I can't—haven't been able to—gauge time, but it seems like every three or four months," Scott said.

Tuan had perfected how to keep the lowest profile possible when talking with Scott. Parallel to the front of the container, a little at a time with each evening's visit, he had carefully scraped the hard-packed dirt away and leveled it so it wasn't noticeable that it was inches lower than it had been. He would stretch out, flat, on the ground as low as he could get with his face next to the opening. "It's likely that they'll move me again, too. At some point, I think they're going to get tired of playing this game, maintaining the charade of re-education camps, and they're going to kill the prisoners they believe could cause them trouble later on. The rest, they will probably let go home. I'll be one of those prisoners that just disappears since I don't have any family to question them or to look for me."

"Do you see any way out of here?"

He knew that Scott was talking about the metal container he was held in. The door was sealed with two thick bars across the outside with massive padlocks. According to Chau, the camp commander had the only key. Other than the ventilation holes, and the opening that they were speaking through, there was just a small opening at the back of the container that faced the deep and wide latrine that served as a foul moat between the camp and its perimeter fence. Every few days one of the field workers on sanitation duty would hoe out the small trench that ran from the container to the latrine. Without a key to the door, the only hope would be to enlarge that outlet for Scott to try and squirm through.

The chances of accomplishing that without getting caught were slim to none. Even getting from zone to zone without being noticed was a problem as each was separated by inner fences of concertina, coils of barbed wire, that the wardens of the camp had strung with metal cans to serve as an alarm system if prisoners tried to cross from zone to zone through the wire. After work hours, the guards closed all the gates, and the prisoners had to remain within their own zones. If they tried to sneak out, there were watching eyes to catch them. Every camp he had been in had plenty of informers—antenna they called them—who watched for opportunities to turn other prisoners in for some reward.

"I don't know, Scott. Sometimes someone manages to escape from a working party, but most of them get rounded up within a few days. The areas around the camp aren't safe, and people that turn in escapees are compensated—it's almost a bounty system and not just in the camps. In the surrounding areas, the villages nearest to the camps, there's always someone willing to sell you out for even the most insignificant of rewards. Some people have so little they become desperate." Tuan's voice trailed off as his mind wandered into thoughts of all that had happened to the people of Vietnam.

"I don't know how much longer I can last." Scott's voice broke Tuan's train of thought, but he didn't sound sad. It wasn't full of despair. He was just merely stating a fact.

From what Scott had told him, Tuan could not comprehend how he had managed to survive this long. It wouldn't help to let him know that so he said to him, "Each day that we live is a day that they don't win. I've heard rumors from new people coming into the camp that some of their family members had made it to the coast and were able to get on boats out of Vietnam to refugee camps in Malaysia or Indonesia. If we can only hang on maybe, something will happen, or maybe the rest of the world will begin to ask hard questions about what's going on with us and thousands of others." He paused but Scott remained silent.

"You told me you were a journalist, right?" Tuan paused again. He wanted Scott to answer and even, more importantly, to start remembering who he had been before April 30, 1975; a proud, honest, journalist who had wanted to let the world know the truth of the war from inside Vietnam.

"Yes, I was a stringer—a freelance reporter—and back then I had a column for the Los Angeles Times. That was a long time ago. Now..." his rasping cough was pain filled.

"That hasn't changed Scott. You are now still who you were then. Someone who has to tell the truth. You're one of those people that survive. And those that manage to get out of these camps and are able to speak about it have a responsibility to inform the world about what's happened here. Don't you want to tell that story?" Tuan heard him sigh, and it was like the release of the deepest, tightest, breath ever held within someone's body.

"Yes. I want to tell that story."

"Then we must be strong. We'll keep living and looking for an opportunity to become free again."

CHAPTER 10

Mid-fall 1978
Barracks 3
Suoi Mau Re-Education Camp

The sun was setting as Tuan entered Barracks 3 after an afternoon of indoctrination. He knew that tomorrow would be far more physically demanding. As he walked through the center aisle between the rows of bunks, he noted that most seemed occupied with only a few that appeared unused and most of those were toward the door where there was the least amount of privacy and quiet. In the far back he spotted Van. He headed toward him looking around carefully for anyone that seemed interested in overhearing other people's conversations. His harshest punishment, at his last camp, resulted from someone reporting an overheard conversation that he had only been peripherally involved in.

"I can't say that I'm surprised to find you in one of these camps, Van. You're a communications wizard, and the communist cadre surely wasn't going to let you remain free."

Van did his own scan of his surroundings and then nodded with a slight grin. "Well, that's not the type of professional recognition I ever wanted. But it's good to see you, my friend." He gripped Tuan's hand and slapped him on the shoulder gesturing at the cot next to his. "I'll get my neighbor here to change so you can have it."

Tuan sat down. "This is my fifth camp, and I've never seen anyone give up their bunk—especially in the back of the barracks—even if it was only to a nearby spot."

Van nodded his head. "He will." He leaned closer to Tuan. "Everyone likes to get the news and..." Van carefully looked around them again. Tuan recognized the process of identification of who was trustworthy, who was suspect and those it was best to be quiet around. Van must have made some sort of indiscernible signal because several men nearby closed in, seemingly at random in their conversations or thoughts, to create an impromptu shield—a wall of bodies screening Van. Who then popped the cover from a cleverly concealed opening in the wall next to the head of his bed. He reached inside and brought out what looked like junk metal pieces strung together with wire. A rusty blue steel razor blade, wire, and crystal, and pencil shaved back to reveal the dark graphite lead protruding from the wooden shaft. "Back in World War II, soldiers called this a foxhole radio... POWs built and used them, too. No power needed." He reached deeper in the opening and withdrew four nails bound together with cloth and wire that had been wrapped around the shafts of the nails and then sealed with wax. He separated them, and Tuan could see that the bare tips of two were configured to hold to your ear so you could hear the broadcast. "It can receive signals when they're strong enough. At night when they are the most powerful, I listen to the news and then share with the others."

In all the camps Tuan had been in, he had never known anyone ingenious enough to come up with something like this. But as much as it heartened him and made him admire Van's creation... he was now, more than ever, scared about what the consequences of discovery would be. He touched the body of the crude crystal set radio with an index finger tip before Van put everything away. That handful of what looked like harmless junk was the kind of thing that would get you immediately killed.

CHAPTER 11

Fall 1978
Outside the Fence
Suoi Mau Re-Education Camp

The two figures ran stumbling in the deepening dusk barely able to see where they stepped but by the feel of the ground under their feet could tell they were still in the cleared field that surrounded the camp. They knew if they could get beyond it to the wooded area perhaps they could elude the patrols and somehow find their way to freedom.

Just ahead, one man called back to the other. "I think we're out of it." His voice echoed as if it came back off the thicket of trees which would indicate that he was right about being close to exiting the minefield. He was winded and couldn't run much further at this pace and felt his spirits lift with the thought they'd almost made it to cover, where they could slow down.

The explosion knocked the second man off his feet, and he felt chunks and strips of some wet, almost rubbery textured, material hit his face and slickly slide down his cheeks and forehead. He wiped them away—the shreds of the other man—and smelled the rich, coppery, scent of blood on his hands. He cried out but not to the man he knew only from having worked side by side with him for months. Both were physically and mentally at what they thought was the end of being able to cope with the camp. He had convinced him the guards were complacent and would not notice the work detail was short by two people. As the guards from the camp surrounded and began to kick him... he cried for himself and wished he had not listened to him.

* * *

THE NEXT DAY
THE YARD NEAR THE CAMP COMMANDER'S OFFICE
SUOI MAU RE-EDUCATION CAMP

Tuan heard he loudspeakers crackle and then quiet to a low hum. He looked at Phu, who had the same look that he felt spread across his face. Camp announcements were never good.

"This is the camp commander." Tuan and Phu were not that far from him, they had just delivered bags of rice to his personal quarter's kitchen, and could hear the reverb of the live sound carrying across the flat plane of the yard and that millisecond of delay as it through the compound's loudspeakers. The voice paused and in the background they heard crying. "A crime has been committed, and punishment must be administered." The speakers popped and hissed for a moment. "Last evening two men decided to not return to their working party. They have refused to become part of the process of rejoining our great, reunified, country and to become a member of our new society going forward. One has already suffered the punishment—late yesterday—for their selfish shortsightedness, and the other is before me now awaiting the same."

They had heard the explosion in the minefield last evening and wondered who had attempted to escape. Apparently, one man had died in the attempt and the other now faced the cruelty of the camp commander. Tuan knew this would not be merely a staking where the commander had the perpetrator of the crime against his rule, his prisoner, lashed to a pole in the yard just outside the commander's office, day in and day out, without food and water. Subject to random beatings until they died from exposure or the abuse. Through the speakers, they heard the unmistakable sound of a pistol round being chambered. The distinctive snick and metal sound it made was not as loud as the shot that followed. The speakers crackled and hissed for just a second more and then they, too, were silent.

That Evening
Outside Barracks 3

"Minh and Trang were from barracks number two." He told Tuan as they mustered for their work assignment. "If they had made it through the minefield, do you think they could've gotten away?" Phu covered a yawn with his right hand. He hadn't been able to sleep after talking with Xuan from barracks two after lights out the previous evening. He had snuck into number three after midnight to warn Phu, who he had known from another camp. "Xuan says they have an informer in their barracks and that they tipped off the guards that Minh and Trang had been talking about how to escape from a working party."

"Then I guess that getting past the landmines wouldn't matter. The camp commander probably had men spread out beyond it waiting for them." Tuan said.

Phu's face rarely lost its usual half grin but did now. "He could have stopped them or announced to the camp that he was aware of a planned escape attempt and that he was increasing security." He shook his head. "That is if their intent really is re-education."

Tuan's laugh was harsh. "He — they — wanted it to happen to make an example and a graphic one at that." He scanned for approaching guards. "They don't care about re-education or unification. They'd be content with the extermination, though, of everyone in South Vietnam that opposed them. It would have disappointed him if both Minh and Trang had died in the minefield. Quan is a sadistic bastard… he wanted one to live and to be part of his public execution." He spat, "They were an object lesson for the rest of us."

A large truck pulled up with its cargo bed half full with shovels and hoes. A second one pulled up behind it loaded with wheelbarrows, bushel baskets, and burlap bags. That meant they would be working the potato fields today. Tuan climbed up on the first truck then reached down to give Phu a hand up.

Settling next to him, Phu grunted. "That would've been much harder three years ago." He pulled his pants up higher on his waist. Once there had been more of him to hold them up.

"Does Xuan have any idea who the antenna is?" Tuan recalled how he had been turned in by one, at his previous camp, and punished as a result. He wasn't sure what he would have done if he had known their identity afterward. It was a possibility he would have done something in retaliation, and then he would likely not be alive to ponder the question.

Phu paused as a half a dozen more men approached and then climbed onto the waiting trucks as the cadre guards and drivers got into their front cabs. With a rough, coughing, sound the engines sputtered as the vehicle exhaust belched smoke and with a clattering rattle both trucks began moving. He leaned to the side toward Tuan did not look at him. "He and others think it's…"

***

THE NEXT EVENING
BARRACKS 3

"Anh, what are you doing here?" Phu caught Tuan's eye and then focused on the man.

"I don't know." The man shrugged. "After today's work detail, we came back, and we were told…" He gestured at two other men standing nearby. "That our new barracks was number three." He shrugged again. "So here I am," he glanced at the men who arrived with him, "here we are." He pointed at three newly empty cots. "Looks like the camp commander must be shuffling people around." He turned from them.

Tuan wondered about the move, too. It might be as Anh suggested but he didn't trust him.

***

Just before lights out, Van and Tuan noticed one of the new men talking with several other of the residents in the barracks. They darted glances at Anh. At first, he did not seem to notice their attention and then, as it continued, he seemed to shift on his cot and become more nervous as their stares and mutters intensified.

The barracks area guard patrol changed shifts right at midnight, and there was a span of time—about fifteen minutes—when as the new team came on watch and the old one off that they rarely were close enough to hear anything in the barracks. Tuan was in that middle area when he finally relaxed enough that he was between sleep and a dream when he heard floorboards creaking in the barracks. He opened his eyes, raised his head to look around and spotted six men who were carefully, trying to be as quiet as possible, approaching the bunk that Anh had selected. Stretching his arm out, he reached over and poked Van

"What?" Even half-asleep Van new to keep his voice low.

Tuan had silently slipped from under his blanket and sat up leaning toward Van's bunk. "Something's going to happen... I think to Anh."

Van sat up, too and followed Tuan's eyes to see the men around Anh's bed. "Well, Phu told me about what Xuan in Barracks 2 said. Sounds like Anh deserves whatever he gets."

"What if they're wrong, what if he's not an informer?"

Van had lowered himself back on one elbow. "Xuan would not make a mistake like that. And why is it that Anh never has to go out on any of the hard working parties?" Van shook his head. "You've seen him yourself just hanging around camp doing nothing but work inside the fence."

Tuan watched as one man at the head of Anh's bunk, who had a rolled up towel in his hands, quickly used it to cover Anh's mouth, smothering his scream of alarm. At the same time, another man at the foot of the bunk and two men on each side grabbed Anh and held him down. Anh bucked and twisted, fighting, against the six men holding him down. But they had him pinned tight underneath his blanket, and he couldn't move more than an inch or two. Tuan then saw several other men silently moving toward Anh's bunk. Some of them held towels, wrapped around heavy objects, that hung low at their side and others were armed with only their bunched fists.

Seconds later he heard the blows start landing on Anh's chest, midsection and lower. His grunts of pain became louder. After a minute, and when his struggles had stopped, the men released them. Just as silently they all returned to their bunks. He listened to Anh's gasps; his painful breathing until he finally fell asleep just before dawn. When he woke up Anh's bunk was empty.

CHAPTER 12

Fall 1978
The Conex Container
Suoi Mau Re-Education Camp

"I was a journalist... a writer." Tuan listened with one ear to Scott and the other for any sounds that meant someone was approaching. The American continued in a low voice. "There was a North Vietnamese Army officer named Bach. He had some sort of vendetta against me, and it wasn't just because of politics or that I was just an American. I think it was because I was an American who fell in love with a Vietnamese girl that he was still in love with. But she had dumped him. Anyway, that last day—April 30th—outside Saigon she escaped on a U.S. Army helicopter with our child, but he got me. He shot me, and as I lay there with his gun at my head, I thought it was over. But the bastard kept me alive—is keeping me alive—just to make me suffer. And to keep it a secret, he has me moved every few months. He's managed to grab some power for himself in some way and can pull the strings."

All Tuan could see was part of Scott's face at any one time through the food slot in his door. Sometimes it was a scarred brow, his eyes in a framework of wrinkles, dirt and lank sweat-matted and crusted hair. Other times it was a filthy beard that hid everything beneath his nose. "After Saigon fell and I was captured I've been moved around, as well. Without a trial. After Saigon was taken, the next day and for weeks to come, the Communists began broadcasting radio announcements across the country that ordered the two and a half million Vietnamese, who had worked for the South Vietnamese government or the United States forces to report for re-education. And at first, it seemed that's what it would be: lectures on communism and the history of their struggle to liberate their country." Tuan rubbed his eyes and listened for anything or anyone approaching them.

"That sounds like the same propaganda they had used in the north on prisoners of war and counterrevolutionary elements since 1961." Scott coughed and cleared his throat. "I went through some of that when I was a prisoner before until they gave up on it and went straight to physical torture to break me."

"Every lecture began or ended with the same statement," Tuan knew it by heart, and it still made him sick to his stomach. "Only if they are closely managed and profoundly educated and reformed can the people of the former South Vietnam live and appreciate the new Vietnam. And only then, will they be determined to have completely abandoned their mistaken thoughts and wicked way of life to rebuild their lives under the new social system."

Shaking his head at words he had heard so many times, Tuan paused then continued. "That's almost an exact quote from the official Army publication that they used. The enlisted men that worked under me and I heard it was for the government workers as well. They were told to leave their homes and plan for a three-day stay for re-education. I and other higher ranking officers and civilian officials were told to bring food and clothing for 10 to 30 days. Many of the people were sent home after a brief time. But I and thousands of others were sent straight to what were either former prisons or military bases that had been converted into long-term re-education camps. Some of the camps held as many as 30,000 people. Here, at this camp, from what I can tell, I think there's between 3,000 and 4,000 men being held here. I would bet that right now, across the country, the Communists are holding at least 100,000 people prisoner."

"I don't understand how they, the North Vietnamese, could convince so many to peaceably enter the—these—camps." Scott's voice had taken on that questioning tone of an investigative reporter.

Even as he described it to Scott, Tuan—despite personally experiencing it—was amazed at how quickly that had happened. "Just a few days, the first week of May, after Saigon had fallen there were the announcements I just mentioned. They started with lower echelon government and military personnel and some of the minor civilian government officials. They were told to pack food and clothes for three days and then report to one of the centers to be taken to a place where they would receive re-education information about what changes would come to the new unified Vietnam. There, they would also learn what was expected of them as citizens of a united country." He paused to shake his head reflexively then realized Scott couldn't see that and continued. "I and others watched hundreds of people go and do their three days and return home. After that first wave of individuals had been processed without anything untoward happening to them, there was another announcement. This was for the upper echelon of the South Vietnamese: mid to senior rank military and senior government officials along with certain teaching professionals from within the educational system. Only we were told to prepare food and clothing for up to a 30-day stay. It made sense, given that we had held positions of higher authority, that they would spend more time on us. I wasn't alarmed since so far, once the heat of battle ended and I had accepted that my war was over, I had not seen or experienced any egregious repercussions or retaliation. And so the following morning I and thousands of others reported to the collection—the camp embarkation—centers. Trucks were waiting to take us to where our own re-education process would begin, and they reemphasized that it would last for about a month. And we believed them based on seeing others, the first to go, report and then return. We thought our re-education might be conducted at a school or one of the university campuses with dormitories where we would be housed. Instead, we were taken to camps that looked more like prisons than they did educational centers. Most of us are still here years later. Possibly the worst thing that happened is that when we reported it immediately identified our families as targets to have their assets stripped from them and to be relocated into the government's new economic zones."

"They really sold it to you didn't they?" Scott's laugh was bitter and harsh.

"I don't know what you mean. What does 'sold it' mean?"

"They packaged it as if it was an innocuous—harmless—part of reconciliation and moving forward. It was set up like putting cheese in a mousetrap."

Tuan understood that. "Yes, and we are still in the trap... most, if not all, of us, will die in it." Now he had a question of his own. "How did you end up here with us?"

"I told you earlier about what happened to me on Saigon's last day. I guess Bach thought it would serve him better, would be more entertaining, to keep me alive. So he pulled the gun from my ear and had two of his men stand me up. One of them pulled out a GI battle dressing and handed it to me. I held it against my side and by touch could tell at least one maybe two of my ribs were broken behind the entry wound. Then I felt a stabbing pain in my back that made me reach behind and around to see what caused it. As I did, it hurt so badly I almost passed out again as my fingers found what seemed like two exit holes' mid-rib cage level on my back. It sounds crazy, but I remember thanking God that the bullets were not still in me. I managed to unwind the gauze pack and then rewrap it around my torso roughly tying it into place. Then I did pass out."

I don't know how much later it was, but when I woke up, the wound on my side and back had soaked through the bandage, and it was crusted with dried blood. When I tried to sit up, I expected it to hurt, and it did. But the worst was the sharp pains that shot through my face and neck. As I lifted my head, I actually felt flaps of skin sag open. My hand raised instinctively to push them back into place. I pressed my palms to them and could feel the blood pooling and fill my mouth. I spat it out. Someone had made ragged cuts from my right and left temple at the hairline and then down across my cheeks to my chin. I lifted what was hanging from my neck and was able to tell it was its skin, large slices of it peeled like bark from a tree trunk, that hung down still attached at the bottom and leaving the muscle underneath exposed.

He—I knew it was Bach who had done this to me—had left a hand mirror next to me on the concrete floor. It's back was now sticky with my blood. I picked it up and looked at my face. I can see where my cheeks had been gashed open; like rough square windows, cut away but still attached at the sill, to view the inside of my mouth. Through them, I could see the side and back of my tongue, and my teeth and jaw were exposed. Then I saw the note he had taped on the wall. Printed in large block letters was: "NO MORE SURFER BOY!"

I heard steps echoing on the concrete outside the cell. I looked up when they stopped, and there he was just outside the black iron bars. He laughed looking down at me. "That's right—no more California beach boy good looks—you think Mai will still love you looking like you do now?" He paced back and forth, his eyes never leaving me. "But I'm going to be kind. I won't put you through ever finding out that she thinks you're now hideous. I'm going to keep you alive but in one of those deep levels—one of Dante's—of Hell. In the new Vietnam, I have the power to make you disappear behind concrete, metal, and barbed wire. I'll make you live in purgatory until I decide you are to die."

I hadn't noticed the camera he carried on a strap around his neck until he raised it and snapped two quick pictures before I could jerk away and turn to face the wall.

"It doesn't matter. I took some when you were unconscious... maybe when I find where Mai is... I'll send copies to her, signed with my love."

He laughed again and then a moment later, I heard his steps fade away. I was still bleeding and weak and fell back asleep or more likely into unconsciousness. The next morning when they kicked me awake I had fresh, but still crude, bandages around my head, face, and neck. Five minutes later I was inside a long wooden box—it looked like a coffin—in the back of a truck full of other boxes headed north. And so here I am." Scott's laugh was more of a grunt. "So you were knocked out, too, late on April 30th in Saigon. What happened when you regained consciousness?"

"They took everything from me, my empty weapons and they stripped me to just a t-shirt and underwear, they even took my boots." He shook his head. "It was crazy. I don't know why they didn't shoot me. When they let me go, I knew better than to go back to my base or the barracks. So I went to a friend's apartment where I sometimes stayed when off duty. He wasn't there, and I never saw him again. I hid there for a few days until they began making the announcements."

CHAPTER 13

Late Fall 1978
New Economic Zone
Near Long Khanh

She never would have thought it was possible—what could be worse than being torn from her family—but things had gotten worse for Lan. The zone commander now outwardly paid far more attention to her than any of the other women and young ladies that worked at the camp. She had heard some of them whispering about how he and other camp commanders were always on the lookout for attractive young girls. And for the first time she thought, maybe that is the answer about why she had been separated from her family.

The Communists had taken everything. Her father, who she knew she would never see again. Her mother, who she hoped one day to be reunited with. Their property and all that they owned was gone and in someone else's hands, now. She was not naïve. She knew that she was pretty. Some even told her she was beautiful and would grow even more so as she became an adult. Now, it seemed the Communists wanted her youth and beauty, too.

At the end of the war all she had thought of was that now maybe she could have her father back and a life together with her family. An ordinary life. Over the past three years, she had realized that would never happen, and she was sure that her country would never be the same for people like her. She dreamed of escaping but had no idea how.

The camp commander was having a party, and she was one of the two or three young ladies who would be serving drinks and attending to guests. His wandering hands and occasional brushes against her had already told her what role he planned for her to play at some point.

* * *

THAT EVENING

The New Economic Zone commander was squat with narrow eyes that never seemed to blink when he looked at her. His looks weren't what made him ugly but what she saw in his eyes and the way he treated the other girls, did.

She saw him step into the hall and knew they would have to pass each other as he headed to his dining room and she returned to the kitchen. As they passed and he was next to her, she felt the hand touch, then caress, her below the waist on her backside. His low laugh disgusted her as he made her pause with his groping and then moved on.

Ten minutes later, she brought a serving platter of freshly carved meat to him in the dining room. She paused as she came in the room not wanting to approach him and looked for an empty spot on the table further away from him. He beckoned her to come to him at the end of the table. He pushed a bowl of potatoes and one of rice to the side for her to put the meat in front of him. She bent forward to lower the platter, and his arm encircled her waist. His fingers again stroking the curve of her butt.

"I think it would be best if you stayed here, in the quarters, as a live-in. It's much better and nicer here than in the female barracks." His grip tightened, and she looked down at him. "I think you'll like it here."

His smile frightened her.

CHAPTER 14

LATE FALL 1978
BARRACKS 3

Tuan had been dreaming of a time just before he had joined the Army. It was in the evening, and he had just left his mother crying in their home. She had lost three sons and a husband to the war already and did not want him to go. He was all she had left. He loved her but could not stand there as she wept and there was nothing he could do for her or say to make her stop.

He had gone outside and started walking, not caring about what direction and without a destination. Head down, he walked hoping to clear his mind. He sensed someone watching him and looked up. There, just ahead of him on the street, was a girl who seemed familiar. She was solidly built but turned from him before he could see her face. He followed her swaying hips and soon they came to a small park. The copse of trees there must have held a nest; night birds on the limbs were warbling and whistling. The sound of them and the sight of her, now standing still, her back to him under the trees, moved him. He walked faster and soon was close enough to reach out to touch her shoulder. Just as he did the low, melodic, whistling sharpened and increased. It was louder, more strident. A piercing sound that made him cover his ears.

It awakened him. The barracks door had burst open, and a half dozen cadre guards had stormed in. One of the guards was blowing sharp blasts on a whistle. "Up. Get up! All of you outside. Now!" He started kicking over cots as others were quickly vacated and the other guards began shoving naked and half-clothed men toward the door and out onto the yard.

Searches of the barracks were not routine and usually only coincided with some incident in the camp or a visit from a government or military official. The latter could never be confirmed—the officials never went beyond the cadre area of the camp—but the commander always made sure to purge the prisoners, and their barracks, of anything prohibited or whose discovery would be damaging to him. The former was a sure thing and far more violent. The staking out or the beating of a camp inmate would inevitably be followed by a punishing search—usually in the early hours of morning—when the men were at their lowest point mentally and physically.

There had not been any recent incidents, and the viciousness of this search was different.

"You!" The guard directly in front of Tuan screamed with his rifle pointed at his chest. He froze as the man rushed him with his rifle now up and one hand on the butt of the stock and the other at the forward part by the sling attachment. The guard slammed into him swinging the rifle butt at his head. "Move!" He screamed again and was so close that spit flew from his lips and landed on Tuan's cheeks. He staggered to one side and saw the guard move past him raising his rifle and aiming at something or someone behind him. "You!" He screamed again. "Stop!"

Tuan watched as the guard clubbed Van away from his cot. The other guards now shoved past him to converge on Van, who had dropped to his knees. They began to kick and beat him with their rifle butts. One of the men, Tuan recognized him as the senior camp guard, stopped and pulled the cot away from the wall. He knew exactly what he was looking for and where it was hidden. His booted foot lashed out, and the cover of the radio's hiding place fell to the floor. The man stooped and reached into the opening bringing out the handful of components Van had meticulously assembled. He dropped them to the floor and crushed them.

Van did not try to look at what the guard had done. Bleeding heavily from mouth and nose, his left eye was pulped and blood mixed with a viscous fluid that flowed from the socket and down his cheek. Tuan had stepped toward him but his look—a white faced weak headshake—warned him off.

Seeing it, one of the guards spun toward Tuan and slammed him in the stomach as another grabbed and dragged him toward the door and threw him outside with the rest of the men from Barracks 3 that were gathered under threat of the rifles from four of the other guards.

An hour later, they were allowed back in. It was nearly dawn. All the cots, but one, had been overturned, and their belongings were strewn about. Van was in his cot. Tuan walked slowly to his friend. He couldn't tell that his face had once been that of a human. A last, rattling, sigh accompanied by bits of shattered teeth and blood came from what had been his mouth. Spilling from his pulped lips were bits of the crushed radio. Van's caved in chest gurgled with a gasp then settled. In the stillness, the only sound was the drip of blood adding to the pool on the floor under him.

CHAPTER 15

THE NEXT DAY
BARRACKS 3

The new man was small and had all of his belongings in what looked to be a dirty pillowcase. It was late when Tuan came into the barracks to find him standing beside the only empty bunk. Van's body had been removed that morning, but no one had rushed to claim his spot. Until now.

"May I use this…" The man gestured at the bunk sitting there bare. Sunlight slanted through the window of the nearby wall casting its rays on a mattress stained and mottled by sweat and blood.

Tuan nodded and watched as the man flipped the mattress over to its less soiled side then tossed his thin cloth bag of meager possessions on the bed and sat down beside it. The man looked up at him and gave him a timid smile.

"My name is Quoc."

That Evening
Outside Barracks 3

"I think we need to be careful about what we say to some of the new people." Tuan looked down at Phu, who squatted with his back against barracks wall that faced away from the Yard and the cadre area of the compound. They could not stay there long because, at some point, a guard patrolling of the Yard would swing around all sides of each barracks.

"I don't know of any that seem suspicious," Phu commented his eyes following Tuan back and forth.

Tuan paced as he talked, constantly scanning for the sight or sound of anyone coming their way. Phu wondered at how he always seemed to be in motion. But then that must come from still being so young and fit like the soldier that Tuan had been. Phu had been a teacher and a slightly out of shape one at that. Finally, Tuan stopped to sit next to him and seemed to settle down. But something was clearly on his mind.

"I've seen it at other camps. Men that gathered information—like antennas on a radio or TV receiver—gathering what evidence that they could about any camp transgressions that they could report and exchange it for reward. Like bounty hunters."

Phu shrugged his shoulders. "In any society that endures or has experienced a regime of oppression..." he paused to push glasses he no longer had higher on the bridge of his nose. A mannerism he had not lost. "There will be some individuals—weak or greedy—that will curry favor with those in authority." He paused to study the young man. "What is on your mind, Tuan? Something is bothering you."

"I was beaten—badly—because of one in my last camp." Tuan grimaced.

Phu had seen the scars on his back but had learned—in the camps—to never acknowledge them or ask questions about what they were punishment for. His friend sat silently with his eyes closed rocking back and forth on his heels. Phu judged the sun's location in the sky, very low on the horizon, soon they must be inside the barracks for the night. For a moment he closed his eyes, too and wondered about the person who had reported him. Was their reward worth the weight that must rest on their conscience? Or did they even have one? He cleared his mind and opened his eyes. "Come, we must get inside for final muster," he tapped Tuan on the arm as he stood.

CHAPTER 16

Early December 1978
Chau's Quarters
Suoi Mau Re-Education Camp

Chau now knew her roommates' routine; the nights when they slept elsewhere. It had never been important to her until now. That first night with Tuan had been almost by accident, but she now wanted more of him and planned accordingly to be with him when her roommates were away, so they wouldn't comment on her own absence, and to be back before their likely return.

That first time with Tuan had resulted from when the camp commander had announced they—the prisoners—would be constructing an area to produce fertilizer for the region's farming and cultivation efforts. Growing food had become a priority across the country.

The evening after the announcement a truck arriving late had delivered their first shipment of raw materials. As the truck backed in Chau looked at Tuan, who had just returned from distributing rations to the barracks. She could not leave the truck unloaded, the driver would return after dinner to pick it up. But she couldn't unload it by herself.

"If we work together, it won't take long." Tuan went to the back of the truck and began lifting burlap bags of raw ingredients from it and carried them to the new area that had been sectioned off for production materials.

Chau climbed on the flatbed of the truck to move the bags to where Tuan could more easily reach to lift them off. She paused with the last bag. "There are a dozen or so five-gallon cans left." She bent to look at a label on one of the containers. "Sulfuric acid," she touched it gingerly then took the handle to lift and slide it toward the back for Tuan. "Careful."

Tuan nodded. He kept pace with her and set them just inside the building's ground-level dock door so that, once unloaded, together they could put them where they should go.

"You're a good worker, Tuan." She could tell he was tiring by the way his arms shook and the tautness in the cords and tendons in his neck. She was exhausted too, as she knelt to push the last one to Tuan. "This is it, and we are done."

Stretching to get his arms around it, Tuan dragged it closer to him then lifted and turned. The canister began to slip, and he lurched forward trying to lower it carefully to the ground. He couldn't hold on, and the container dropped the last foot to the rough concrete floor. When it hit a badly joined seam around the top came free, and a spray of brown liquid jetted out splashing across Tuan's right thigh.

"Damn!" Tuan hissed and began pulling at his pants. The cloth had already started to blacken and smolder.

Chau jumped from the truck bed and grabbed her canteen as Tuan yanked his pants off. A palm-sized patch of skin, high on his thigh, had already turned bright red. She knelt and poured a handful of water on it.

Tuan gasped. "Wash it off... Hurry!"

She turned the canteen and emptied its contents over the burning flesh of his thigh. She carefully touched, then stroked, the unmarked skin about the raw patch of tender flesh. His breathing deepened as she moved her hand slightly. His erection began to grow beside her fingers. She reached, timidly at first, to touch him with just fingertips then more surely her fingers closed around it, and she stroked the shaft.

"The door." Tuan's low voice moaned.

The truck was now empty—unloaded—and she could... should... shut the door. The driver would come back and think them gone. She pulled the door closed and turned off the large overhead light leaving them in the dimness of a distant, single, light bulb dangling bare from the ceiling at the very back of the building.

She returned to Tuan and did not need the light to find him and to continue what she had started. It throbbed in her hand as she sensed his stomach muscles tense and his back arch. "Come with me," she let go and took his hand. She led him to the small room to the right of the doors that had turned into her private work area. On its floor was a pallet of blankets that she sometimes slept on when she found her quarters and roommates too depressing to be around. She lighted the Coleman lantern—salvaged from a U.S. military unit—and in its yellow glow turned to Tuan and unbuttoned her tunic. Her nipples were erect, creating twin tents in the thin fabric of her undershirt. They ached to the touch, but all she could think about was how good his hands and then lips would feel on them. Completely naked now, she grew moist as she watched him take his shirt and then his undershorts off, working to disengage his hardness from its folds. The ridges of his stomach muscles, so well-defined by the low-calorie diet, were highlighted by the low angle of the light. He lowered himself to her. His hands. His lips. They burned her skin with a delicious languor. She tasted him as he did her. Soon the slow pace became frenetic, thrusting and an unbearable need to reach their apex—one that each sorely needed. They crested at the same time, and as they lay there, each with their thoughts tumbling around, their skin glistened under the lantern's light.

* * *

The Conex Container

Scott's first worry was for Tuan. "Are you sure you can trust her?"

Tuan had given the situation a lot of thought deep into many nearly sleepless nights. "If they find out they could—likely would—kill me. But..." He spread his hands in a 'so what' gesture that Scott couldn't see. "I'll never get out of the camps anyway. Might as well make things better right now, in this one." It was quiet for a moment, and Tuan heard the call of guards across the Yard. He did not have much time, and he would have to go soon to make night muster.

"I'd likely be dead by now if it wasn't for you." Scott had not fully realized it until that moment. "I had given up. And if you hadn't talked to me and made me feel like there was at least one person to listen to me—to make me feel alive—then I could not have gone on."

Tuan felt, for the first time in more than three years, that sense of responsibility for another human being. He thought that emotion had died, as others had, with his unit—his men—that final day in Saigon. He had given Scott a reason to keep fighting and to stay alive. And maybe had needed that too because he had felt himself slipping to the point where nothing mattered anymore. Now, if something happened to him Scott would truly be alone, and he would die. "Maybe her helping me will lead to somehow being able to help you."

"You mean to escape." Scott coughed.

Tuan rubbed his eyes. He was a fool. Where could this thing with Chau lead? Nowhere. She would be redeployed, or he would be transferred. Or they would be caught and shot. That was all he could expect. He couldn't keep the doubt out of his voice. "I don't see how, though."

Scott's voice seemed stronger. "It doesn't matter Tuan, get all you can from it—from her. But be very careful."

CHAPTER 17

MID-DECEMBER 1978
THE YARD
SUOI MAU RE-EDUCATION CAMP

"Do you know where the news—from the outside—comes from?" Quoc had asked Tuan that before.

Tuan watched the working parties forming and was, again, thankful that he was no longer on any of them. Materials close to the camp were getting scarcer, and they were sending them farther away to work, which made for an even longer day. He looked back at Quoc, who somehow had managed to get one of the easier assignments, to go around and clean the camp each day by picking up trash and other refuse. "What did you hear before you got to Suoi Mau?"

Quoc shrugged, "I heard so many things and don't know what's true and what's not. That's why I wonder where people in the camp are getting their news."

Since Van's death, Tuan never talked to anyone, other than Phu, about what had happened or was going on in the world beyond the compound's fence. He watched as Quoc, who shrugged again when he did not reply, moved off toward the cluster of other prisoners near barracks four. That was his first stop in the circuit of all the prisoner barracks that Tuan had seen him make of the camp every day since he had arrived. Tuan headed to his own morning routine at the storage building to sort out the daily breakfast rations under Chau's supervision. He would then return to the building in the evening for delivering the dinner portions around the camp. As he approached the building, he saw a familiar figure pushing his empty wheelbarrow. The way he moved showed he would never become entirely at ease with physical labor.

Phu stopped when he saw Tuan so he could catch up to him before he entered the yard where the materials were stored. "Rocks or sweet potatoes today?"

Phu straightened but still had to grin up at him. "Picking up sweet potatoes, today." He rolled his eyes at the storage building. "Thankfully."

Tuan looked in the direction of barracks four and thought about Quoc and his questions. "What do you think about the new man?"

"Who... Quoc?" Phu followed his look but knew better than to let the wheelbarrows legs touch the ground when it was empty. In some uncanny way that always brought the guards immediate attention—something always best to avoid—so he kept it up and walking slowly kept it rolling. "He seems okay. He's quiet and seems to enjoy listening."

Tuan knew that anyone who would sit still and listen to Phu would be considered an okay guy in Phu's evaluation. "What do you mean, he listens?"

"He's always hanging around when others are talking but doesn't say much. He just listens. I like people who don't speak too much."

Phu was a brilliant man yet seemed not very self-aware at times, but he struck Tuan as also a good person. "Just be careful what you say to him. Remember what I told you the other day." He paused and patted Phu on the shoulder before stepping into the storeroom.

"What do you mean?" Phu had a puzzled look on his face again.

"Nothing, just that it pays to be cautious sometimes." Tuan waved at Phu as he turned his wheelbarrow to the left and toward the row of other prisoners queuing up for the work detail.

CHAPTER 18

MID-DECEMBER 1978
A STONE QUARRY 20 MILES FROM SUOI MAU

Phu slowed to bring one hand up to wipe his forehead only for the sweat to still run into his eyes. The labor warmed him and even in the chill air, he perspired heavily. He missed having Tuan with him on the working parties. There were others to talk to, but he knew Tuan actually listened to him. Thoughts of Tuan always made him think of how his son might have turned out if he had lived. Watching his country ripped apart—all the years of bloodshed and the death of so many men, women and children—was still not as painful as the unhealed wound from losing his wife in childbirth.

If his son had survived, he would be close to Tuan's age. But then, if he had lived he certainly would have been compelled to go into the military and then faced a likely, terrible and frightening, death. To taste life in all its splendor and yes, even its moments of bitterness only to lose it so soon. So many of his countrymen, young and old, had experienced that—a life ended so abruptly—dying before their time. For that to happen to his son would have been a burning Hell even worse than the one he was in now.

Still shaking his head, he bent to his work. The guards were more heavy-handed than ever since Van's death and had beaten—would beat—prisoners for the slightest infraction of camp rules or provocation.

* * *

THAT EVENING
BARRACKS 3
SUOI MAU RE-EDUCATION CAMP

As rough and Spartan as the barracks was, it was still a relief to step inside it at the end of the day. Despite the smell of too many men in a too small space, with limited ability to keep themselves and their clothing clean, and that the cycle of backbreaking physical labor would start all over again with the sunrise. Never mind that the relative quiet of the evening and what sleep they managed in the night was spent hungry. Always hungry, with a yearning anticipation for breakfast, as meager as that was, growing as the evening ended and night turned to dawn.

He nodded to several of the men as he sank onto his cot with a sigh. His dinner had been quickly eaten. A handful of rice and a small sweet potato, one of the most blemished—with large rotted spots—he had ever had the misfortune to receive. He had closed his eyes, like most of the men and put it in his mouth chewing and swallowing it as fast as he could without choking. It was awful, but it was all they were given.

He glanced toward the back of the barracks to see if he was there. But he knew Tuan would likely still be with Chau. That made him both pleased and worried for his friend. Though his stomach hurt, thoughts of what he had seen early that morning troubled him far more.

His eyes went again to the back of the barracks. At the cot next to Tuan's—formerly Van's—sat Quoc. It didn't seem like he was watching anyone in particular but his eyes, roaming the barracks, kept coming back toward him. Phu's stomach spasmed, and he prayed it wasn't another onset of dysentery. Quoc knew that he had seen him that morning as he came out of a building and was followed only moments later by someone he had thought looked like the camp commander, Quan. Phu could not see clearly that far away without his glasses so he could not be sure. No prisoner—not one that lived, anyway—had ever met personally with the camp commander or got even near him. When the two left the building, each had moved in opposite directions but Quoc's own destination had brought him toward Phu. He did not pass close, but Phu just could not turn his eyes away, and he came near enough to soon recognize him. Their stares locked as he kept walking and he knew Quoc realized that he had witnessed his meeting.

Quoc stood and stretched. He didn't look in Phu's direction, but his feet brought him closer. He stopped next to his cot and nonchalantly looked down. Phu didn't stand but tilted his face up and met his stare. He saw his usually placid face tighten, and though his mouth grinned, the smile didn't show in Quoc's eyes. They were hard and glinted darkly. His lips straightened as he leaned down.

"Eyes and mouth should never join together, right my frien-"

Tuan's arrival cut him off as he sat next to Phu and clasped him on the shoulder. "how was today?"

Phu flinched and then half turned to greet his friend then looked at Quoc, who had straightened with the smile returning to his face just like a person who puts a mask on for a party.

"It is so good to have a friend like Tuan, isn't it Phu?" He nodded at Tuan. "Someone to talk to... but only as long as you don't tell them too much." Quoc's smile broadened as he nodded again, this time to both of them and then turned away to join a cluster of men near the door.

"What was that about?" Tuan shifted to turn toward Phu.

Phu shrugged his shoulders and then grimaced. Pain lanced through his side and through his stomach. Cramps. He managed a grin for Tuan. "Who knows. Quoc's an odd one."

Tuan saw the sweat beading on Phu's forehead though the evening was cold. "Are you okay?" He reached for the canteen hanging from his bunk's corner post. "Here, drink some water." He lifted it to hand to Phu.

"No. I'm fine." Phu waved the canteen away and then rubbed his stomach. "Just a touch of stomach trouble. But I think I will lay down, now. We'll talk in the morning." Tuan returned the canteen to the post and with a concerned look left him. Phu stretched out and through half-closed eyes saw that Quoc still watched him.

* * *

It was an hour before dawn, and Phu could not hold it any longer. His night jar was already full so he rose from the tangle of his sweat soaked blanket and stood shakily. The cold sweat chills racked him as he carefully maneuvered past sleeping men to the barracks door. It—this gut wrenching pain—was not uncommon and had happened to others in the night and they had done what he was doing. Though it was prohibited, he opened the door and stepped silently as possible outside, around the corner and a dozen feet away to the latrine behind the barracks.

Squatting with his buttocks just over the edge, racked by the chilly night air on his sweat-slimed skin, he felt the sudden gush of hot, fetid, fluid stream from his body pumped out by the cramps that contracted his stomach and sphincter muscles. Eyes closed, he couldn't help but gasp at just that single moment's relief. Awareness returning to him, he heard the crunch of footsteps, opened his eyes and looked up. It was Quoc and with him the big guard who had found Van's radio. Tuan had pointed him out afterward and warned Phu to be careful around him.

In the lightening sky, he could see the glint of teeth behind Quoc's derisive grin. "I don't trust that you can keep your eyes and mouth from working together."

"But I couldn't see that far... my eyes..." Phu gripped his pants and tried to stand and protest.

* * *

Tuan yawned and stretched. No matter how tired he was when he finally fell asleep each night, he always woke before most of the others. He sat up and as usual looked to see if Phu was still sleeping with this thin blanket pulled up to his chin. But he wasn't there, which was something that had never happened since their becoming friends. He scanned the barracks and didn't see him. He slipped his shirt on as he stood with pants in his hand. Barefoot he walked toward Phu's cot. The two men next to it were sitting up now.

"Ca... Mai An, where's Phu?"

Both men shrugged and rubbed their faces. They looked at the empty cot next to them. "Not there."

Tuan swallowed the words he was tempted to say in reply. Carefully with his right foot, he slid the night jar out from underneath Phu's cot. His nose twitched and crinkled, the pots all smelled foul even when you were used to the stench. This one was near to overflowing. "He must be at the latrine." Turning from them he went back to his cot, pulled his pants on and slid his feet into open-toed rubber sandals made from an old tire.

Two minutes later he stood looking at a body face down in the latrine. "Hand me that." He told Ca who had followed him out and pointed to it. With the rake, he managed to roll the body over. It was Phu.

"He must've passed out, fallen in and suffocated." Ca whispered not meeting the look Tuan gave him.

Tuan's voice was harsh. "Look at his face." He grabbed Ca and pulled him closer. Even through the filth, they could see Phu's eyes had been gouged out.

CHAPTER 19

SUOI MAU RE-EDUCATION CAMP

Tuan had heard the stirrings within the camp but what caused them came from without. Some of the newest prisoners, coming in from other camps, had been able to collect information from their families during rare visits. Others, inmates who were technicians—Van had been only one of them—had been assigned to repair the camp's radio and electronic devices for the commander and guards and were able to listen to broadcasts from Voice of America and the BBC. They were so excited by what they had heard that sometimes at night they snuck from zone to zone and shared the news with others in the camp. Tuan was concerned that they were so eager to share anything positive that they exaggerated it. But the news seemed promising. The latest report was that the United Nations had accused Vietnam of Human Rights violations and was demanding that the communist government release all political prisoners.

It had become a nightly routine where Tuan lingered after delivering his rations and filled in Scott on the news and what had happened after his capture and imprisonment on April 30, 1975.

"We had been prepared in advance for an evacuation order. At the end, I was assigned as a military liaison with the U.S. Army and knew what to expect. But I was still amazed at what I saw April 28, 29th and 30th." Tuan whispered.

Scott shifted around and brought his hands up to his face to trace the ridges of the ragged, poorly healed, scars down the sides of his head. They ran from his temple into the dirty, tangled, beard, with its bare spots where the hair would no longer grow. They were jagged trenches deeply gouged into both sides of his face. "I remember the 30th and watching the last helicopter..." It was that last night in Saigon when Bach had given him those scars. They didn't end with just his face. Flaps of skin had been torn, peeled, from his neck; it had been partially flayed and pulled down, in strips, to his collarbones. He remembered tearing his shirt into strips that had quickly become bloodied bandages trying to hold pieces' flesh back in place. Pushing that memory back down deep, he crouched closer to the opening and could hear Tuan's steady breathing just outside.

"The U.S. and South Vietnamese Army and Air Force helicopters filled the air over Saigon like a flock of birds. I held my position as I had been ordered to as the North Vietnamese approached. My ammunition was gone, and my men were dead. Mortar or a grenade, I'm not sure which, exploded near me and knocked me off my feet. As I lay there half unconscious, I watched them. At first, they seemed like birds circling over a dead body… then I realized that they carried the living. And that those of us there on the ground that remained behind… we were the dying. We were the dead. I remember that there was no noise of war, no screams or shouts of victory from the North Vietnamese that were now right on top of me. It wasn't playing then, but I heard it just the same. It echoed through the streets. It was that song, White Christmas by your singer Bing Crosby. It was the last thing I heard, and then I passed out."

They both were silent and lost in thoughts and memories neither wanted to have. Scott broke the silence.

"How are you getting any current news?"

Tuan shook himself and realized he must go soon. "Before he died, Van had worked on the camp commander's radio. So many things are falling apart and into disrepair, and the cadre doesn't have the technicians to fix everything. When he was testing his work, he caught part of a Voice of America broadcast. It said that the United Nations is calling for an investigation into human rights abuses by the new

Vietnamese government." Dirt picked up by a gust of wind sprayed across Tuan's face, and he wiped his eyes clear of it. He was close enough to see that Scott backed away from the opening to avoid getting a face full of dirt, too.

"What do you think? Is it true... will they—the United Nations—investigate?" Scott coughed.

"Van thought so. He had heard enough other news on his radio set to corroborate it. So it might be true, but I don't know that it will change anything anytime soon."

"Even so, that's a good thing, isn't it? But you sound worried. Why?" Scott asked.

"It's so encouraging that I'm worried some of the prisoners will do something rash or stupid. And all that will do is lead to reprisals and locking the camp down even tighter."

* * *

THAT EVENING
BARRACKS 3

After his talk with Scott, Tuan thought long into the night. He knew how intoxicating good news, especially heard stealthily or illicitly—in complete rebellion against authorities—could be. It sometimes led you to excess and carelessness. He remembered talking with

Phu late one evening when neither could sleep despite being tired—just like this night. Their minds would not let them rest. He had asked Phu how he had ended up in the re-education camps. He had been a professor at Saigon University. Tuan had learned that surprisingly for someone who seemed so good-natured and always ready to smile, Phu had been targeted because of his activism and minor rebellions. That and his love for South Vietnam and hatred of the aftermath of the war the communist cadre called *unification*, got him sent to the re-education camps. He closed his eyes and could hear Phu's deep voice:

"I had a small radio in my office, and I would sleep there to catch broadcasts since signals were stronger at night. I would periodically wake up to check different stations and channels. I would so carefully turn the dial incrementally and slowly hoping to catch the BBC or Voice of America. When I did it wasn't news, not really, about Vietnam—the U.S. and it seemed the world had moved on from my country. But they talked about the greater world outside it. Everyone was living and experiencing things that I knew I'd never have in my own country. At least not in what my country had become. Though I used to live for each one of those sketchy, static-filled broadcasts; I was deathly scared I would be caught listening."

"But you weren't?" Tuan commented. As much as Phu enjoyed talking, what had happened to get him sent to the camps was something he had never spoken about.

"No," Phu's usual smile was gone. "Not in the act of listening… but one night I fell asleep under my desk with my radio on with my headphones over one ear. One of the other staff members found me that morning but didn't wake me. They brought North Vietnamese soldiers to my classroom. They woke me with the muzzle of an AK-47 under my chin. I felt its cold metal and heard the low static hiss in my ear until the headphones fell from my head as I crawled out to stand in front of them. I watched as the officer wrote a note on a sheet of paper and instructed one of his men, 'take this to the person who led us here.' The soldier saluted and left. I knew the note he carried must be details of how the person who reported me was to be rewarded. I never found out who that was… I spent that night in a jail cell at a local police station and the next morning was sent immediately to a camp in the north."

The memory had not helped Tuan relax so he could rest. All it had done was make him think of his dead friend and of Van, too. So many ghosts crowded his thoughts that Tuan felt he would never be able to sleep peacefully again.

CHAPTER 20

CHRISTMAS EVE 1978
NEW ECONOMIC ZONE
NEAR LONG KHANH

Lan was finishing the work that Kim hadn't; she had disappeared some time ago, leaving everything for her to finish. If the work wasn't done, she would be the one punished. She straightened from stacking pots and pans underneath the counter and though young she was exhausted. She had risen at 4:00 AM to begin her day and it was now 10:50 PM. She took off the wet apron that had soaked through and now her blouse was also wet. She put the balled up apron on the counter and took a handful of napkins to wipe her face, neck, arms and upper chest inside her blouse. She sighed and closed her eyes, yearning to sleep but dreading waking to another day here, to this. She opened her eyes.

The camp commander was standing there, in the doorway, watching her. He seemed closer than he actually was. Startled, she stepped back. The man entered the kitchen and came closer.

"Still working?" The man asked backing her into the pool of light created by the single light bulb that hung over the kitchen's prep table. She tried turning away. His eyes never left her as he picked through the assortment of knives in the butcher block knife holder on the counter. "Too small," he sounded disappointed. He reached into his back pocket and withdrew a large knife. With a loud snapping noise, he unfolded and locked the long, serrated, blade in place. "This is much better. It helps with girls who don't want to cooperate."

His bulk blocked the light as he came within arm's reach of her. A gust of wind rattled the window over the kitchen sink and its rumble and howling wind smothered her cries. The light through the glass poured week watery light onto them as the blade glinted.

"I've watched you for months." He now had her pinned against the counter. "Tell me you want me," he twisted the blade, holding it in front of his eyes and admiring its sheen, "now--." He grabbed, got a handful, twisted her long dark hair, and waved the knife over her stomach. She reached behind her and found the handle of the rolling pin she'd used earlier and not put away. Screaming, "No," she swung and connected with the left side of his face. She heard a cracking sound as his cheekbone broke, "you bastard!" He backed off a step, and she kneed him in the groin. His scream was louder than her gasp as she grabbed the knife he had dropped and in reflex, she stabbed the blade through his throat. Choking in his own blood, he slipped to the floor arms clasped over his chest.

"Good!" A shrill voice came from the doorway.

Lan spun from looking down at the zone commander's body, the butcher knife still stuck in his neck.

"He disgusted me," Kim stepped into the light, "but I had it easier here if I let him do what he wanted, when he wanted, to me." She had her arms wrapped tightly around her chest. Lan saw the shudder she controlled as she came closer and stopped beside the body. She looked down silently for a moment then she viciously began kicking it in the ribs and then face. Finally, breathing heavily, she stopped and turned on Lan, who, startled, had backed further away from her. "Then you came here!" She quickly bent, grabbed the butcher knife and pulled it free from the body and with a lunge slashed at Lan's midsection in a single motion. "I'll kill you, and they'll find yours..." the flashing blade slung thick clots of blood from its length, "with his." She twisted to give the body another kick.

Lan continued backing away around the center table that was used for preparing food until it was between them. Kim turned to her, stepped to the table and shoved it into Lan, knocking her against the counter behind the table. As Lan bent forward, her long hair swung free. Kim had come halfway across the table after her and grabbed a handful, yanking it toward her and down to slam Lan's head onto the table top. Dazed, she got her feet up against the counter behind her and gripping the table's edge kicked off. The power of her legs shot the table and Kim backward. Letting go of Lan's hair, she stumbled then, as she tried to regain her footing, fell over the commander's body. She went down hard striking her head on the concrete.

Lan scrambled over the table and landed on her knees and with her full weight on Kim's stomach. She heard the whoosh of air as it was punched out of Kim, who didn't move. Gasping she grabbed the blade from her hand. Shaking, she held the tip to Kim's throat. I could kill her, she thought. The tremors reached the hand holding the knife. It jittered enough that the razor-sharp tip touched and then danced sideways. Lan blinked, collected herself, and seeing the thin two-inch cut began to bleed, she dropped the knife. Crying and shaking even more, she knew she had to run. But to where?

CHAPTER 21

CHRISTMAS EVE 1978
SUOI MAU RE-EDUCATION CAMP

The population had grown tremendously since he had arrived. Tuan estimated that the camp now held nearly 10,000 prisoners. He and several other inmates in the K-1 zone had planned a celebration for Christmas and decided to invite prisoners from the nearby barracks. At 9:00 PM they began to arrive at Barracks 3 to join the party. It had been decorated with a nativity scene, a large cross, altar and other decorations. At first, it was a quiet, somber, evening but after a while several conversations, then heated arguments, broke out about the secret news of the United Nations demands and how that might possibly mean their freedom.

This is bad, Tuan thought. The guards are going to hear. He walked among then pleading, "Please, be quieter. You must be silent." But they didn't listen to him. He moved to the back of barracks, away from the cluster of men grouped around the holiday decorations.

Twenty minutes later, the barracks door burst in. Three cadre camp guards with rifles entered. They didn't even warn them to quiet down. Instead, they fired a volley of shots into the ceiling. Then two of them covered the crowd of prisoners as the third tore down the cross and destroyed the altar and the nativity scene. That punitive action, coupled with the news they had heard, enraged and emboldened the prisoners. They attacked the guards and took their rifles. Tying them up and leaving them in the barracks they spread throughout the camp, managing to overcome other guards and acquire more guns. Singing Christmas songs, the mob surged through the camp and took control of most of the zones.

Tuan knew that as bad a decision it was by the prisoners, this was the moment, the break, he and Scott had been waiting for. But he also knew it would not take long for the cadre to regain control and put down this small-scale revolt. And the punishment and reprisals would be severe.

Not even slowing down to try and take a gun or rifle for himself, he ran for Scott's cell, crossing the zones and not worrying about the noise from the rattling of tin cans tied to the wire. Scott's container cell was in an area where people were running through but not lingering. It was either clusters of guards racing toward the prisoner zones or prisoners rushing toward the cadre compound. As he slid to a stop beside the concrete block storage warehouse adjacent to Scott's cell, he realized he didn't have an answer for how to get him out. He should have grabbed a gun. He ran to the cell door and dropped to the ground in front of it. He could see a pale gleam of something in the opening that had to be Scott's face trying to see out or hear what was going on outside.

"It's an uprising, Scott. Some of the prisoners have guns, but this won't last long."

"Tuan, you have to make a break for it. You can't get me out, but you have to escape. If you do and can make it out of the country or to the U.S., let the State Department know about me and please try to get in touch with Mai at the address I gave you in California. It's a long shot, but please try."

"No. I'm going to take a gun from one of the guards and come back to shoot these locks off." Tuan flipped the top one, and it clanged against the metal.

A circle of light illuminated him and the door of the cell. "What are you doing, Tuan? Do you want to be killed? I mean…" It was Chau. She had a rifle slung over her shoulder and was holding a pistol in one hand and a flashlight in the other. "I was coming to see if I could find you in your barracks to make sure you were okay." She was shaking.

"You have to help me. Let me have your gun and flashlight." Tuan stood and approached her.

"What? Help you do what and what do you want the gun for?" She stepped away keeping the light on him. "Are you crazy? I'm taking you back to your barracks."

"I have to help him."

"Help who?" She seemed close to turning and running away.

Tuan used the only leverage that he had and even though it was necessary he felt a qualm at doing so. "The man inside is an American. He can help us. He can get us into the United States. You've told me you don't have any family and how many times you've thought about going to America. But you knew you never would be able to. Well, this is that chance. Inside that container is an American journalist, if we free him and can get out of the country... asylum and a new start in the United States are the rewards."

"We would be together?" Chau asked him, her eyes wide, their brightness caught in the rim of light from the flashlight.

"Please turn out the light and give me your gun. I need to shoot the locks off." He moved closer to her and took her in his arms, it was the only way. "We will take you with us. We can get out of the country."

"Together?" He felt her arms tighten around him.

He thought of Scott dying in a metal box. He thought of his own life wasted and spent, what was left of it, in a never-ending cycle of camps and prisons. He said what he needed to say to have this one small chance to change that. "Together. We'll go together."

She nodded and handed him the pistol. Quickly, his two shots were lost in the sporadic volleying of other gunfire ringing out in the darkness around the camp. Tuan soon had the locks off and pulled the door open. Scott was on his feet, but Tuan could tell he was weak. He staggered forward, coming out of the container and Tuan caught his arm.

"We have to be strong and live to tell the story, right?" He had his head down and seemed reluctant to look up—and then he did—at Tuan and then Chau.

In the flashlight's beam, Tuan saw a face that had been mutilated, the lumps and rough seams of poorly healed wounds that left what must have been a once handsome face disfigured. He had almost flinched but caught it in time and instead smiled for Scott and then looked at Chau, who stared at Scott with a frown and revulsion. He nodded at Scott and held onto his arm to support him. He motioned to Chau, "Let's get out of here."

* * *

Thirty minutes later they had passed through two inner gates without any problem. As they approached the third Tuan noticed it was manned by a heavy guard, the plumpest he had seen in three years in the camps, and when Chau saw him she stiffened and stopped. Scott, who was trailing behind her, also came to a halt.

"What is it?" Scott coughed and tried to cover the wheezing sound as he caught his breath. Tuan could see he was tiring.

Tuan ignored Scott and turned Chau to look at him. "What's wrong? Keep moving."

"I know him… He was a sergeant, and I was under his command at one time—in one of the other camps. I reported his misconduct, and he lost rank. He's not going to let me or us pass without…" She shook her head.

"What kind of misconduct?" Tuan asked.

She looked at him and without her saying anything he understood. "Okay. I hate to ask this but can you distract him?" He could see that she was beginning to doubt what they were doing just by the way she looked at Scott then back at him. He took her arm, gently, and pulled her to him. "I need you to do this… for me… for us."

She looked up and nodded. "I'll do it… but for you not him." She shook her head at Scott then straightened the line of her utility uniform pulling the blouse so that it hugged her tightly across the chest. As Tuan led Scott into the shadows that ran along one of the sentry houses she approached the guard. The guard passed his flashlight up and down her lingering on certain areas. She moved so that he would turn his back to the shadows and focus on her.

Tuan worried that the look on her face would give them away as he motioned for Scott to stay still. Silently he crept up on the guard from behind. She was talking to him in a low voice as he got the chokehold on him and with a vicious twist that resulted in a crunching sound he broke the guard's neck.

CHAPTER 22

CHRISTMAS DAY 1978
NEAR THE CAMP COMMANDER'S OFFICE AND MAIN GATE
SUOI MAU RE-EDUCATION CAMP

Tuan knew Chau was frightened, but she had managed things well so far. It was in the early hours before dawn, and the chaos of rampaging prisoners was behind them, but they faced an even greater problem. Lights swept the field from the watchtowers and from flashlights carried by the guards flooding into the camp. The staff buildings and commander's quarters were alight, and men scurried in and out of them.

Tuan, Chau, and Scott squatted in the shadows of the large classroom used for re-education lectures for new prisoners. They were near the main entrance and the exit from the camp. Minutes ago, the sweep of an arc of light had illumined the patch of ground in front of the classroom, which was situated exactly as he had seen in his first camp where the man had died on Tuan's first day in the communist's re-education system. Tuan blinked away the surreal vision that he might be only minutes away from dying in a very similar spot. He wondered if they would let his body lie there, too—an example to the rest of the camp. He looked at his companions and thought he would probably be the fortunate one of the three. He didn't want to think of what the communist cadre would do to Chau for helping them and Scott, the American, would likely be torn to pieces.

Scott breathed heavily, coughing more, as he leaned against the wall then slid to the ground. So far he had kept up with them, albeit with Tuan's strong arm helping him along. The weather was a cool 66°, not cold but he was shivering and felt the rattle deep in his bones. They needed to keep moving and get clear of the camp and find some clothing for him and Tuan. He looked at him and hoped he had some sort of plan even if it was hastily formed. They couldn't stay in one place, certainly not where they were, for long.

Across from them, next to the main gate, was the guardhouse that checked everyone coming into the camp. Just behind it was a door-size frame for a smaller entry and exit to and from the camp without having to open the much larger main gates.

"There..." Tuan touched Chau's shoulder to get her attention. "That's how we get out of here."

Chau looked where he pointed. "It's manned — see him through the window—at all times. How will we get by him?"

"We," he looked at her then at Scott. He had no idea if Chau had it in her and knew Scott was too weak to be much help. "I will have to kill the guard at the gate."

She looked at his bare hands and knew that as strong as he was compared to the other prisoners, against a well-fed, armed and alert guard he wouldn't stand a chance. "You are crazy, Tuan." She scanned the darkness around them and followed the stab of spotlights directed behind them, across the Yard penetrating deep into the camp toward the barracks area. "Let's stop this right now. We can turn back, and I'll get you…" She paused to glance at Scott, "back to your barracks safely." She looked again at the American and shook her head before turning again to Tuan.

He stopped her before she could continue. "There is no going back." He sighed and prepared himself for what he had to do and worried that she would ruin it intentionally. "I have an idea… listen to me…" As he told her, in the glancing, cast-off, illumination of a spotlight, her eyes widened.

"You really are insane." Chau sounded more the communist cadre and less his lover. "That will certainly get us killed." She gripped his arm, and he felt her fingers dig into his forearm.

Tuan put his hand on hers to free it and then stroked her cheek softly. "It's the only way." His voice was quiet and steady. He knew that there was no way Scott would go back into that metal container and that he would peacefully return to the barracks. That was not living; he would be dead just as he would likely be if what he proposed to do failed. He looked at Scott and explained to him what he had just told Chau and what she had said to him. "You understand what to do?"

"Yes." Scott nodded. "But she's right about it being crazy." He paused and rubbed his face not dropping his gaze from Tuan. "But something this foolish is probably the only chance we have."

"Chau?" Tuan looked at her. "You have to do this for all of our sakes." He saw her eyes dart to Scott. "Think about if we can escape and become truly free in a country that gives us the opportunity to make a good life." Her eyes were back on him, and her face softened. "Together."

"I will do it..." Her eyes flicked at Scott then back to him.

***

Five minutes later, Tuan was in position and watched them as they passed through several small pools of light between them and the guardhouse. When the time, and Chau and Scott's position, was right he would have to run faster than he ever had to cover the distance.

Rifle over her shoulder, Chau had the pistol leveled at the back of Scott's head as she marched him toward the guardhouse. Tuan heard her call out, her voice loud and clear, as she got closer to it. "Sentry—Sentry! I need your help."

A large figure moved from within it and stepped out into the light cast by a single bulb light fixture over the door. Something about him seemed familiar to Tuan as he readied himself to sprint at his target. All that he had for a weapon was the heavy flashlight he had taken from Chau earlier. He knew he could kill with it if he had to. He was aware that in just minutes, he would.

"What is it, comrade?" The guard lowered his AK-47 but put a hand on the holstered gun at his belt. "Who do you have there?"

"I found this man crawling through the shadows toward the fence." She gave Scott a little, unplanned for, shove that made him stagger half a step and almost try to turn his head to look questioningly at her.

"Near what barracks?" The guard had taken a step closer to them then stopped still well under the light.

"I don't know," she hesitated then continued. "I don't think he was in a barracks."

Chau and Scott were now only ten steps away from him.

"What barracks are you from?" The guard harshly directed the question to Scott.

Chau shook her head and replied. "He won't answer me." She moved Scott closer but half-circling around the guard and not directly to him. Under the light, the guard turned with them his eyes now locked on them and away from the cluster of buildings across from the gate. Chau now brought Scott directly to him and stopped two arm's lengths away.

With the light and the guard's attention fully on them, Tuan took off just as Scott exclaimed, "Merry Christmas mother fucker," and straightened to reveal himself. Under the light, even with the long dirty hair, matted beard and scars his face was still distinctly American.

Shocked, the guard hesitated then brought his rifle up just as Tuan hit him from behind slamming him forward. Scott dropped to the ground in front of the guard wrapping his arms around his ankles. The man fell. Hard over Scott's back. Tuan held the flashlight mid-shaft and brought its base down on the back of the man's head as he followed him to the ground. The sledgehammer below at the base of the skull where it curved joined the neck must have crushed vertebrae.

Tuan felt it crunch as the metal struck thin skin and bone. The man did not move.

Gasping, Scott managed to slide from under him and stand. Barely. He was swaying on his feet, and Tuan quickly rose to steady him. "Help him inside the guardhouse," he called to Chau motioning at Scott. She hesitated and then took Scott's arm to lead him into the small shack.

Tuan grabbed the guard's ankles and dragged the body in after them. Flicking the flashlight on he saw the face of the guard, a thick thread of blood had run from both nostrils and into his mouth. He checked him again. No pulse. He looked at his face under the flashlight's beam. It was the guard who led the killing of his friend Van and likely had something to do with that of Phu's as well.

"I know him." Chau looked away from the body. "That's Truc. He's the senior guard and a personal friend of camp commander Quan."

Tuan began to strip the body. The man's clothes would be a loose fit for him but much better than the prisoner rags he wore. He saw that Scott had remained on watch and scanned the gate area while he dressed. He grabbed the dead man's cap from the floor where it had fallen, put it on, and looked at Chau. "Is there anything useful inside here?" She didn't move from where she stood looking out toward the commander's office. "Chau!" She stepped over to the standing desk and shuffled through it.

"A couple of maps and another flashlight." She handed them to Tuan.

"Someone's coming!" Scott's voice was hoarse but clear. He shrank back in the darkness of the corner trying to get low and out of sight.

Tuan stood in the doorway, the guard's uniform cap pulled low to cast a shadow over his face. He watched the man approach scurrying through the lighted areas and sliding to a stop in front of the guardhouse.

"Truc," the man hissed and then called again louder. "Truc!" The man's head pivoted around watching behind him as he turned and came closer. "I'm glad it's you on duty during an alarm. Help me. Some of the men from the barracks suspect... they will... they will kill me. They are following behind... not far."

Without talking, Tuan waved him into the guardhouse. The man scampered in like a cockroach escaping the light. "Thank you... I knew I could count on you." The man stopped as he looked up into Tuan's face. "You're not Truc!" he cried.

"No. But you are the man responsible for the murder of my two friends." Tuan hit Quoc in the face with the pistol knocking him to his knees. He called over his shoulder at Chau, "get Scott to the exit gate and outside… I'll join you in a minute." Hearing the crisp tone of his voice, Chau did not hesitate. Tuan only had to wait for a moment for the sound of machine gun fire nearby to cover the single shot that came from within the guardhouse.

CHAPTER 23

Christmas Day 1978
Just North of Bien Hoa

In the chaos and surprise of the uprising, Chau had been able to get them through the area immediately outside of the camp. The field around the camp gate had been cleared on both sides of the road and even further beyond, where it arced to merge with the minefield that bordered most of the camp. They didn't know, but it could have been mined as well. They needed to put as much distance from the open area as possible and find a place where they could catch their breath and plan what to do next. After a quarter of a mile the cleared area ended, hopefully marking the end of the minefield, and they were able to get off the road and into the cover of trees and underbrush. The road ran directly into the main highway, and they could not stay in proximity to it for long. Patrols would be heavier on it and the likelihood of someone spotting them far greater.

Tuan had heard the rumors, and part of the news others had heard, about refugee camps set up in Indonesia and Malaysia but didn't know details. Getting to them meant finding a boat, which meant they must go south. But the communist cadre would know that as well and would be looking for refugees headed to the southern coast.

It must've been shortly after daybreak when they stopped. They had seen a convoy of military trucks carrying troops on QL1 the main highway close to the camp. They knew that soon the camp would be locked down and with daylight, a search for missing prisoners would spread out over the area. Chau had come from a northern province, moving south with her unit as the North Vietnamese Army advanced, and knew little about the area around Suoi Mau and Bien Hoa.

Tuan looked at the patch of woods and thick scrub brush that shielded a low area from the sight of the road. "We'll need to stop here and wait out the day. It's too dangerous to be moving around in broad daylight." He looked at Scott, who had had been the first one to drop to the ground when they stopped. "And we all need to rest." He ignored Chau's scornful, darting, glances at Scott as he scooped away rough grass to make a hollow to stretch out in. He searched his memory for places to hide and some, out of the way, course they could take to get them to the coast undetected and hopefully find a boat to take them from

Vietnam. The places that immediately came to mind were all to the south, and he knew they would be the first places searched. They had to do something that the cadre would not suspect. "We have to go north." He looked up at the overcast sky and was thankful for it. He waved at them to move closer to see and hear him better.

Chau was shaking her head so sharply that her cap came off. "No!" She flattened out beside him.

Scott had caught his breath and asked, "Shouldn't we go west, maybe into Cambodia, or South? If we can get to a radio, maybe I can get a message to an American. Maybe there aren't any U.S. forces in Vietnam but you can bet there's some in the region, and there are sure to be U.S. Navy ships off the coast."

Scott looked completely spent. Tuan could already see that they would only be able to move as fast as he could allow them to, but leaving him behind was out of the question. Tuan shook his head and looked at them. "I don't think we can get across the border and into Cambodia—things might be even worse there—and if we immediately head south for the coast, we will be going straight into the area where the cadre is going to have the most troops, and informers, looking for us."

"What do you mean, if we go immediately south… what's your plan?" Scott had leaned against the trunk of a tree and closed his eyes.

"The only direction for us to go that has a chance of us not getting caught quickly is the one they wouldn't expect us to take. That means north, but not far, just enough to where we can curve around and then head south. By moving slowly and patiently, we won't look like escapees, and when we turn south, by then, maybe the search will have spread out, and the troops won't be as concentrated so that we can slip through them." Tuan studied Scott and even in the spotty moonlight could tell he was not Vietnamese. That would be the first thing they would need to do. Disguise him in some way.

"What about him?" She was thinking the same thing. Chau pointed her finger at Scott.

Tuan smiled to put her at ease, something he did not feel but he had to calm her. "We are going to steal some clothing for all of us, and you are going to help me make him," he gestured at Scott who and opened his eyes, "look like an old Vietnamese man."

Scott laughed and sat up straighter with a groan. "The old part won't be too difficult. I think I can easily move that way convincingly."

CHAPTER 24

December 26, 1978
Camp Commander's Office
Suoi Mau Re-Education Camp

The camp commander had enough to deal with and did not want to take the call. But he must. To not pick up the phone would set off a chain of events that would make matters, as bad as they were already, far worse for him. It had just happened a mere day before. How had this man heard of the outbreak and that his special prisoner had escaped with the aid of one of his guards!

He waved the clerk away from his desk, the note she had given him still in his hand. "Out and shut the door!" He picked up the phone and heard the buzz and line noise of their pathetic—countrywide—telephone system.

"Yes, sir." He said into the mouthpiece as he took a deep breath. He sat in his chair but did not slide back into his usual slouching pose when talking on the phone. His body was tense and had been since he was awakened by a panicked aide and the camp alarm several hours ago.

The man's voice was surprising, remarkably steady as it always had been. "Commander--"

"I promise we will find them, sir!" He blurted cutting the man off.

"Find who Commander? I'm calling to have a man—you know which one—moved tonight. It's time." The line was silent except for a small crackle and pop. "Commander?"

He felt paralyzed and unable to speak then managed to stutter. "I... I..."

"You what, Commander?" The voice now had the icy tone of someone who could kill without regret and make people—entire families—disappear without remorse.

"I... There's been an escape. A revolt—an uprising—in the camp. Some are missing."

"Who is missing, Commander Quan?"

He swallowed twice and still the lump in his throat hung there. "Your man, sir."

Static on the line increased in pitch and when it finally lessened he heard what he had expected and dreaded.

"I'm coming to Suoi Mau." The line went dead.

The commander stared at the phone in his hand and wondered how long before he was too.

The Next Day
Camp Commander's Office
Suoi Mau Re-Education Camp

Commander Quan wasn't expecting such a young man. It didn't take long before he realized that this man—his senior in rank—though young was deadly to anyone who crossed him or that thwarted his plans. And Quan had let escape someone, a prisoner, that figured largely in those plans that this man was not finished with.

"How did this happen?" The man's voice and the tone were quiet and cold.

Quan swallowed the bile in his throat. "Guards broke up an unauthorized gathering-" The look on the young colonel's face made him stop.

"A gathering? What kind?"

"A Christmas celebration—the guards--" the man in front of him raised a hand, palm out, to stop him again.

"Your guards, commander. They are your guards."

Quan swallowed again and nodded. "They tore down the decorations in the barracks, and that set the prisoners—I mean the men in re-education—off. They took rifles from the—from my—guards and tied them up. They then spread to the other barracks, attacking other guards across the camp."

"How did my prisoner get free? He wasn't in one of those barracks, was he?" The menace wasn't in the words or the question but in his flat tone and that his eyes darkened and pierced the camp commander. They held the promise of a knife thrust if he didn't like the reply received.

Quan shook his head. "No, sir. Of course not. One of the... one of my guards says that he saw what looked like an American POW accompanied by a female cadre guard and a male prisoner headed to the camp's main gate during the uprising." He paused and then hastily added. "He was under attack and could not go after them, sir!"

"So my prisoner had help?" His look and tone lightened.

"Yes, sir!" Quan nodded so vigorously that his carefully combed hair now hung down over his brow.

"And they managed to get out of the camp and to escape?" The deadly tone had come back into the young colonel's criminals voice.

Quan's nod was slower and more careful this time. "Yes, sir. Once we got the camp locked down, we did a headcount, and identification cross-checks of all the prisoners and also my staff and guards. Missing were one female cadre member—in charge of supplies and material, one male—a former South Vietnamese Army officer..." Tuan paused. "And your man. The locks had been shot off the Conex container that he had been held in."

The colonel coldly gestured for him to stand. Quan did, and as the man moved around behind his desk, he stepped aside for him. The young man sat down. He was silent and didn't move for a moment and then with a vicious sweep of his arm everything on the desk was shoved onto the floor.

"Bring me the female cadre's and male prisoner's personnel folder." He reached for the phone. "I'm going to set a bounty, a reward for anyone who can lead us to them or can provide information that helps to capture them." He looked up at Quan and his dark eyes glinted. "When we get them back—and we will—there is no reward for you... but you might avoid the harshest punishment I can devise for your failure." He started dialing, paused and looked up at Quan, "get me those files now!"

CHAPTER 25

SIX MILES NORTHEAST OF BIEN HOA

It had been slow going. Tuan, Chau, and Scott had paused and stopped several times waiting out what they thought sounded like men or patrols moving on the nearby roads and areas adjacent to them. It was near sunrise as they followed an overgrown path that led them away from the road. In the growing light, he spotted it. The small house, barely more than a shack, was set far back where it couldn't be seen from the road among the high scrub brush and a patch of trees. The rundown shanty seemed forgotten; perhaps the owner had died somewhere else... alone. Tuan wondered how many of his countrymen had died that way.

Inside, they found leftover scraps of clothing and near an overturned washbasin, a rusty straight razor and a small dried-up piece of soap. Tuan picked up the washbasin. "I saw some rainwater in the ditch. I'll be back shortly, and we'll get you cleaned up." He motioned at Scott's dirty, heavily bearded, face. "See if you can piece together any of that clothing or scraps of it to make something for him." He looked at Chau, who seemed reluctant. "Please, help him." As he went out the door, he saw her picking up pieces of fabric and material from wads of them on the floor.

In the morning sunlight Tuan moved quickly, now able to see as he hurriedly filled the bowl and moving more slowly, saving most of the water from spilling, returned to Scott and Chau. "We shouldn't drink it, but it's good enough to wash up with." He set it on the rickety table and picked up the razor and soap. Not trusting Scott to have a steady hand and unsure of Chau's mindset, twenty minutes later he had Scott's beard trimmed leaving several bloody nick's and cuts. Once cleaned up, his scars were even more ghastly and the thought of such hatred it would take to do that to another human chilled him.

Scott was now wrapped in a body length light gray blanket that looked like an old man's shawl. On his head was a battered nón lá Chau had found half-crushed in a corner. The conical hat was held in place with another strip of gray cloth that wrapped around the hat and was tied under his chin. It would serve in the near dark of twilight, but there was no way they would be able to move in daylight without a better disguise for Scott and different clothing for him.

Tuan had not noticed it before, but Scott's right hand had been crippled. The fingers and the thumb bent at odd angles—like bent and broken jackstraws.

Scott noticed Tuan's look. "The man who did this..." Scott gestured at the scars on his face and neck. "When he turned me over to his men to take me a camp in the north, he told them I was a writer. So at the first opportunity they gave this," he held up his right hand, "some particular attention."

* * *

"He will hear you," Tuan whispered to her, hoping she would let it go and that once she saw Scott as something more than an escaped prisoner—and as a human being — she would accept him.

"He's asleep." Chau looked over at the darker shadow slumped on the ground but only six feet away. She did not care if he was awake and listening. "He's a danger. If we're caught, we might be able to bluff our way out of it. Or I can claim I followed and captured you." She hesitated and repeated, "it's better to leave him and go our own way."

"I won't go back into one of their camps, Chau." He put his arm around her. "There are probably a hundred thousands of Vietnamese fleeing, or trying to flee, the country." He gestured toward where Scott slept. "I believe he is a good man and--"

She cut him off. "How can you say that? His people are responsible for a war that ripped our country apart!"

"He's one man. Not a government and North Vietnam is equally to blame..." He sighed as he felt her stiffen. "Leaders of all the governments and their high-ranking military are responsible. Not this man. Look what's been done to him!"

"He's dangerous to us." She pulled away from him, and he withdrew his arm.

Tuan sat straight no longer leaning toward her. "I have to help him. If we can get out of Vietnam to a refugee camp... you understand that him being with us means more attention. We won't be just two people among thousands of Vietnamese hoping to find safety and an opportunity in the United States."

She didn't answer him so he closed his eyes and leaned back against the wall hoping that sleep would come soon. Nightfall was just a few hours away, and then they would move as fast as they could. They needed to keep moving. He could feel the pressure of the soles of Chau's feet against his thigh. She had curled up on the ground beside him. By her soft breathing, he could tell she had fallen asleep. They were both tired and soon his own joined with hers.

Scott listened to the sounds. He was even more exhausted than they were but had not been able to sleep. As weary as he was, what he had just heard stoked the fear already growing in his mind. That he was just a bargaining chip if things went bad for them and they were caught. He understood Chau's feelings. Raised in a communist country under an unforgiving doctrine how could she feel otherwise about him. And Tuan? Scott thought he was a good man, too. One trying to do the right thing. But he worried that at some point he would change and being good would lose out to self-preservation. If that happened, there would be no hope for him.

CHAPTER 26

December 27, 1978
Near Chùa Vân Sơn

They had made slow but steady progress under the moonlight. It was nearly dawn, and they needed to move from the side of the road and into the woods to try to find someplace to sleep through another day. As they came around a rising bend in the road they saw the salvaged American Jeep, it's hood now painted with a yellow giant star on a red background parked on the far side of the crossroad. The two men—North Vietnamese army soldiers—sitting in it must be checking travelers on the roads. Tuan didn't know if it was routine or special because of the uprising at the camp and that had put the entire region on alert. He suspected that was so, but there was nothing they could do. The men had already spotted them and were no longer reclining sleepily in the Jeep. One had retrieved his rifle and other had a hand on his holstered pistol as they stood in the road. Tuan bent and whispered into

Chau's ear. "Just tell them we're walking your grandfather to the next village to catch the next bus to Ho Chi Minh City. Don't stop and we'll all keep moving." They were too close now for her to answer him so she nodded.

As they got alongside the Jeep, she nodded at them. "I hope that the sunrise is the end of your long watch, comrades and that you rest well. As soon as I walk my grandfather and cousin to the bus station I plan to, it's been a long night." She opened her mouth with a jaw-cracking yawn.

The shorter man closest to the Jeep stretched, too, and nodded. The taller one relaxed, taking his hand from his holster, as he clearly recognized her North Vietnamese dialect and glanced only briefly at the military ID card that she held out as they passed them.

Twenty minutes later, they were far off the road and settled down behind a chest-high pile of fallen logs. They scooped out an area beside it and toward the woods just large enough where the three of them could lay underneath. Using a scrap piece of canvas that Tuan had found on the side of the road to cover them they raked leaves and dirt on top of it to hide their sleeping spot. The only way they would be discovered is if someone walked directly on them. Tuan handed them a canteen of water to drink from and soon they were all asleep. "Tomorrow we need to cross the Dong Nai, we need to be on the other side of the river."

* * *

THE NEXT DAY

In the small village, just across the river, they had stolen the bundle of clothing that Chau carried. They had found the dried clothes on a line strung behind the largest hut closest to the massive bushes that grew into the tree line.

By Tuan's calculations, they could follow the river to the edge of Hồ Trị An, a vast lake he recalled visiting as a child with his family, and then cut across and head more east than southerly. They needed to swing wide and away from Saigon, now referred to as Ho Chi Minh City on the maps they'd taken from one of the guards at the camp. He looked up from that map and saw Scott pulling on dark, drawstring, pants that came close to fitting his length along with a loose pullover shirt of the same material. They were much better than the rags he'd been wearing though those had been covered by the rough blanket draped on him like a shawl. They were getting into an area of increased patrol activity so clothing that would stand closer scrutiny was definitely needed. To bypass the villages and heavy traffic and connect with the road due east they would have to cross several miles of open fields and throughout them was a network of dirt roads and paths. He checked to make sure Scott had adjusted the conical hat, lowering it to cover most of his face. "Okay, let's get moving."

Thirty minutes later, he looked back over his shoulder at Scott, who was trailing again and seemed to be moving slower. They would need to rest soon.

"Tuan!"

Chau's cry made him spin around. She was as far ahead of him as Scott was behind. His eyes followed where she was pointing and in the bright moonlight—nearly the equivalent of visibility at dusk or dawn—he saw the cluster of uniformed men and jeeps ahead of them at the edge of the copse of trees. One man, probably an officer, was standing on the hood of the vehicle with his binoculars trained on them. Tuan knew there was no way they could escape a closer inspection. "Chau…" He gestured at her to come back to him. Scott caught up with where he stood at the same time as she. "I have to lead them away and get them to chase me."

Chau was shaking her head. "No! You can't do that."

"If we stay together, we can't outrun them." He saw the look that she gave Scott. "It's not his fault. I need you and Scott to head to that wooded area a few miles back and hide. I'll lead them away in the opposite direction." He pulled out their two maps. "I'll meet you here," he pointed at a grid location on one of the maps and handed it to Scott, "48 hours from now. If I don't show up, head south and east without me taking this route." His finger traced a major highway headed toward to the coast. "If I'm able to, I'll try to rejoin you somewhere along that road, hopefully."

"I can't let you do this, Tuan." Scott grabbed his arm. "Let them take me and you and Chau escape."

"Yes!" Chau nodded and implored Tuan. "I won't go… not with just him."

He shook his head. "The only way this will work for any of us, is if we get Scott to American authorities alive, don't you see that Chau?" He pointed back the way they had just come. "Get going." He took out Chau's pistol and chambered a round. With a last look at them, he ran angling toward the cluster of men at the edge of the field and then away and into the fields that rolled to the horizon.

CHAPTER 27

LARGE FIELDS NORTHWEST OF LONG KHANH

Tuan had moved faster on foot through the rough fields than the Jeep, which the patrol wouldn't abandon. By crisscrossing the wide ditches and irrigation channels that eventually ran closer toward the thick undergrowth leading to a dense tree line he had ducked into the woods once he was out of sight.

He had been leading them north when had finally managed to lose them. Turning east and south he was now many miles away from where he, Scott and Chau had been when the patrol first spotted them just before dawn. It was now early afternoon, he could run no more and needed to find a place until nightfall. Deep in the brush, he burrowed down to hide. He took a last look at the map and traced the route he had given Scott and Chau to follow.

He knew he must make that rendezvous or Scott would be quickly abandoned at best or turned in by

Chau at worst. He hated the daylight and barely slept as he waited for sundown.

* * *

Lan had been born and raised mostly in Saigon or its outskirts, she had no idea where she was headed but was running there as fast as she could. She knew once they found the commander's body they would be scouring the area for her or anyone that looked suspicious. That meant she must stay off the main roads and not travel during the day. She saw the first rose-colored tint of the sun rising in the sky behind her as she turned into the trees and began looking for someplace where she could hide until nightfall. The field that she was in, unlike several others she had already crossed, was overgrown and pockmarked with what looked like bomb craters many of which had half filled with water. She prayed that she had not strayed into a minefield. She knew about those from a girl in the zone camp whose brother had died in one.

Up ahead, the first slanting rays of morning sunlight showed a dilapidated, half falling down, shed or small barn between two patches of trees surrounded by heavy undergrowth.

She opened its creaky door to a pitch black interior. Moving carefully inside, a step at a time afraid she would fall over something, she moved deeper inside until her outstretched hand struck what must be the back wall. At her feet, she felt a pile of something that shifted as she stepped on it and her sneezes told her it was dusty and dry. She stooped and carefully raised a handful to her nose. It had the sour smell of old plants or moldy hay. The pile was deeper in the corner as she followed the wall with her hand. Kneeling in the corner, she scooped out a clear spot and burrowed under leaving an opening for her face so she could breathe. She was so exhausted that the rank smell did not matter, and soon she was fast asleep.

She awoke to the noise of the door opening, it's creak and rattle the same sound she had caused when she entered. Someone was inside the barn with her. She heard their breathing and the muffled sound of slow steps coming closer. Then she made the mistake of trying to hold her breath, instead drawing in a nose full of dust that made her sneeze and cough.

A cone of light came on and spotlighted her. It was a tall man and in the glow of the flashlight, Lan saw his own young, scared and sweaty face.

"Who are you and what are you doing here?" Tuan asked her.

* * *

The girl who had finally calmed down enough to believe that he wasn't going to hurt her or turn her in... had just finished telling Tuan her story. And at its ending, his statement that she should come with him was met with hesitation. She did not want to.

"If you don't come with me, where will you go?"

She shook her head. "I need to find my family," she paused at the thought, "my mother... she's all I have left."

He had seen so little of her face because she kept it bowed and turned away from him, but she sounded young. Through the gaps in the wooden slats of the wall, he could see it was growing light outside. He knew they were in for a miserable day confined inside the dusty, smelly, shed. There was time to talk with her and convince her that her best chance of survival was to come with him. She looked up at him, and he saw her young, beautiful, tear-streaked features. "If you search for your family, you'll be caught, and there is no telling what will happen to you. You've seen how some men, who now have power over us, have treated you. Do you want to gamble that any others you meet will act differently?"

* * *

They had made good time. It was still an hour before daybreak. The girl had kept up with him and been even quieter in her movements than he. "Wait here." He motioned for her to stop as he moved ahead. They were very close to the spot where Scott and Chau should be.

Not more than a hundred feet from them, just off the road, he saw where they would likely have camped. He came back and brought the girl with him to study it to be sure. Within a minute he had spotted them before they saw him and the girl. He gave Scott the whistle that they had preplanned to let him know that it was him and that he was going to approach their hiding spot. As he stepped into the small clearing Chau rushed to embrace him.

"Looks like you brought a guest... Or a new friend." Scott grinned, relieved to see Tuan. His face, even with the grotesque scarring, was more relaxed and less careworn.

That brought Chau's head up from Tuan's chest to look behind him. "Who is she?"

Scott could feel the heat and anger in her tone. Tuan sensed it as well and attempted to head her off. "This is Lan. She escaped from one of the new economy zone camps where she was being abused by the commander."

"She must go... She can't stay with us."

Tuan followed Chau, who had taken three steps away from him but closer to where Lan stood unsure about coming any closer to Scott and Chau. "She has nowhere to go, and I've promised to take her with us to safety."

"She'll be safe somewhere else, other than here. She must go!" Chau was white faced, angry and getting louder.

Scott scanned the area searching for any movement nearby and trying to hear any sounds other than night birds settling down for the day.

Tuan put his arm around Chau. "Lan was being raped by the camp commander and managed to escape. There's nowhere for her to go and no place that is safe for her except with us."

Chau had calmed down but was still shaking her head. Scott looked at her and then Tuan. He knew there would be more trouble over this, but he agreed with Tuan the girl was safer coming with them.

CHAPTER 28

EAST OF LONG KHANH

"Where are you from?"

Lan only knew a few words of English and looked at Tuan, who translated for Scott. She brushed a long strand of hair from her face and tucked it behind her ear. "Saigon." She ducked her head but raised her eyes to Tuan. "Originally... now..." she shrugged her shoulders as Tuan passed that on to Scott. She darted a quick look at him and wondered what his own story—the one behind that horribly scarred face—was. She had seen many American service men and just like the Vietnamese boys and young men she had met, some were handsome and polite, some were even charming, and some were crude and ugly. And the ugliest were those who at first seemed good looking and friendly and then showed their true character.

This American—Scott—sounded nice. He had smiled at her though it twisted his scars into an odd shape on his battered face, and he and Tuan appeared to be friends. The woman, who was still glaring at her every time she looked her way, looked far uglier to her, but that was because of how she had reacted to her.

"She and her family lost everything when they relocated them to one of the New Economic Zones." Tuan told that to Scott and turned to repeat it in Vietnamese for Lan and Chau. Chau still acted as if she didn't care one bit for Lan.

* * *

JANUARY 1, 1979
NEAR BẢO BÌNH

Chau watched Lan, who unlike her was willow thin and graceful as she bent to scrape cooked rice into four small bowls. Her scowl made Lan's smile drop when she handed one of them to her. Chau took it without thanks or acknowledgment beyond her harsh glare.

A gracious and grateful smile returned to Lan's face as she walked around the small fire that they had shielded behind stone and brush with a piece of frayed canvas draped behind it on the side toward the road they had left an hour before. She sat closest to Tuan, between him and Scott. Each of them hungrily emptied their bowls. Lan turned to Tuan, "Thank you for taking me in…" Her eyes went to Chau, who ignored her, and then she turned to Scott. "Thank you all."

"We have enough to slow us down." Chau gave a sideways look at Scott. "You better be stronger than you seem to keep up with us."

Lan instinctively knew that Chau meant herself and Tuan, not Scott. She caught Tuan's eye, "Would you tell him, please" she pointed at Scott, "that I thank him, too. My family has—had—many American friends from my aunt's work at the embassy." Tuan had told her about them all the day he met and had convinced her to come with him. She studied Scott's face in the waning sunlight. The scars were horrible, and he had such pain and misery in his eyes. "Please tell him I'm sorry for what has happened to him."

"Sorry!" Chau's tone was unforgiving. "His Air Force—American bombs—killed my mother."

"Too many on all sides have died," Tuan eyed the darkening sky and stood to kick dirt on the flames. "It's time to go." He made sure the fire was completely out and pulled the tarpaulin off the bushes, folded and put it in his pack. He slung that over his shoulder as the others gathered their packs. "We are all," he glanced meaningfully at Chau, who avoided it, "in this together. We need each other."

CHAPTER 29

WEST OF LONG GIAO

Scott had asked Tuan to look for a notebook or notepad and pens or pencils when he and Chau were out scavenging for food. It looked like he had found one. As Tuan emptied the canvas bag, he had been using to carry what they had scrounged, he set a purple and pink, what had to be a girl's, diary on the ground next to him.

Scott picked it up and opened. He found that other than some pages at the very front it was blank. He noticed that Lan had risen to stand by Tuan, and she looked at it with a wistful smile. Scott held it out to her, and she tentatively took it and opened at the beginning. He saw her eyes moving as she read and soon her smile faded. She closed it, and he saw the tears in her eyes. Then she bent her head and turned away sobbing quietly.

"What's wrong... What's in it?" He looked at Tuan.

Tuan took it from him and began to read:

"April 14, 1975—My aunt brought me this though my birthday is not for another two weeks. She works at the U.S. Embassy in Saigon and said a friend there had brought it for her all the way from America. She smiled as she gave it to me but afterward, as she was talking with mother, they both looked upset. Mother has not smiled much since father died but now she seems very scared.

"April 28, 1975—My aunt is here for my birthday. She arrived in the night. When I went to breakfast this morning, as I came into the kitchen, I heard her tell mother that the Americans were leaving. Tears were running down her cheeks as she looked up when I entered, and I wondered why. She continued to talk to mother, 'The Communists are coming. They will take Saigon and like locusts will take everything we have.' Mother calmed her but looked at me as she replied to her, 'We will adapt, and we will survive.' My birthday was spent in fear of something I did not understand and that my mother and aunt would not talk about. I went to bed but couldn't sleep. All night I've heard trucks on the road. In the evening they had gone north but now, late night into early morning, as I write this it seems far more of them are headed south."

"April 29, 1975 — More trucks moved south throughout the day but by late afternoon, there were not any on the road. It was still, and I had never seen it that empty. Just before evening, I heard a rhythmic clanking as if it looped around and around. It was accompanied by a rumble of engines—some seemed to be shifting up and down. I knew that distinctive sound from driving with my father in his truck. It got louder as if what was making the sounds was getting closer. In the distance, I heard gunfire and an occasional boom like an explosion. Mother pulled me away from the window as it all soon grew quite loud. Our window glass along the front of the house rattled, and mother took me to the back of our house away from the road. She held me as we laid on the floor against the back wall. I felt the floor and wall vibrate with the power of what we hoped was passing us by. I felt my mother's tears drop on the left side of my face as I pressed the other against her chest and I was afraid. I didn't cry, but I thought of a story I had just read about dragons... vengeful dragons used by evil men to destroy what they didn't take from the land they had recently conquered. I know that they couldn't exist in the real world, but a part of me wondered if what I was hearing and feeling came from them.

"April 30, 1975 — This morning I saw mother outside, looking to the south. Her eyes were on the sky, and I followed them to see the black specks moving in the distance over where I knew Saigon to be. Then I heard a fierce beating of wings behind and above us. Again I thought of the dragons I had read about as I turned to see, only to have to pitch my head straight up then back as I turned again to follow the large dark helicopters flying low and fast toward the city. When Mother took my hand, I saw that she was no longer crying. As the sound faded, she hugged me and whispered, 'We will survive.'"

Tuan looked up at Scott. "There are many pages loose, and some are gone." He continued, "May 5, 1975 — They came slowly through our streets — the jeeps with a giant gold star on a red background—on the main highway outside our home was a man with what mother told me was called a bullhorn. How funny that name. He was telling people that worked for the government or with the U.S. military that they would be required to report for re-education and that announcement and further instructions were coming."

Tuan paused, "More pages missing," then continued, "June 18, 1975 — When I woke this morning, I heard mother speaking with someone. She was in the family room with a man in uniform who held a clipboard in one hand, the other with a finger extended marking the spot on the top sheet of paper. Mother was telling him, 'I said my husband is dead. Here is the letter from the Army and one from an American officer he was friends with, about his death.' The man checked the documents and made a note on his paperwork. He then noticed me, smiled and turned back to my mother. 'Is this your daughter?' Mother paused and then answered. 'Yes.' Her eyes warned me to be quiet and a quick tilt of her head in the direction of my room I took to mean to leave them. As I did, I heard him tell her, 'She is so young... and so pretty.' The tone of his voice made me shudder."

Tuan shook his head, "A lot gone here." He aligned the loose pages and continued:

"July 20, 1975 — It has been quiet for the past week but many of our neighbors—men mostly—are now gone. Uncle Hung, not a relative but our closest neighbor and my father and mother's best friend who made kites each spring from paper bags for me and my friends even when the fighting was heaviest, had told my mom that because he worked as a mail carrier, he'd been told to report. He's now been gone for days, and I know there will not be any kites flown this year. Despite the people leaving and not coming back, mother seems better.

"A gap here. It looks like she didn't write anything for a while." Tuan was holding several of the loose pages in place as he read. "August 1, 1975 — I'm writing this as mother packs. She is hurrying because the man from the other day weeks ago is back. He has documents that say we must move now. Taking with us only what we can carry. She just told me to put this— my diary—away. I didn't look up as I want to get this all down. Her sharp cry did make me see if she was okay. I then saw what had startled her. The man is now in the room with us. As I write this, he is staring at me. I will not look at him. He just told my mother that the new place we were being relocated would give us an opportunity to become part of the new Vietnam. He said everything was going to be okay. Mother knelt there, clothes and her picture album before her to try and find room in the last suitcase. The man was standing over her but was looking at me as he said, 'I'll check on you personally.'"

Tuan aligned the loose pages and closed the diary. For a moment he stood still with his head bowed before handing it back to Scott. "That's the last entry."

* * *

It was the first time she had opened up and talked freely with them. Lan's voice was quiet but steady. "I learned that living in the country was vastly different than just visiting it. My father and mother had lived in cities or just outside them all of their lives as had their parents. They had cousins who lived in small villages—in the rural areas—far from real towns and once we visited some of them when I was very young. But that life and how hard it was day in and day out was not anything they had experienced and neither had I." Lan looked at Tuan, who translated it for Scott.

Tuan watched him as he slowly, a grimace on his face, printed his notes left-handed in the diary he had found for him. As they had settled down until nightfall, he had taken it out and asked him to ask Lan some questions.

"Thanks," Scott nodded to Tuan. "Please ask her to describe the day when she was taken to the New Economic Zone she was moved to."

Tuan turned to Lan, who replied to him but looked at Scott as she spoke. "She asks, the first one or after they separated her from her mother?"

"The first zone camp but it's important I hear about what went down when they came back to take her—by herself—to the other area. And what happened there."

The grim look on Tuan's face showed that he knew some of that story from Lan or maybe similar ones from other people whose families had been forcibly relocated and in some cases families that had been torn apart. He repeated for her what Scott said and as she answered him, with pauses, retold the story to Scott.

"My mother and I were loaded into the back of a truck filled with a dozen other people, mostly women with their children. We were only allowed one bag each. I remember my mother cried quietly. One woman who wailed loudly, causing her small children to cry, as well, was roughed up by one of the guards. He swore at her until she quieted her children. My mother's tears were silent. They ran down her face to drip off her chin.

I wept too but was equally still. I wished and hoped I could help her. Before being ordered — then escorted— from our home, mother walked through each room touching, sometimes stroking, what we were leaving behind. I think that is what she cried for and not out of fear of what was ahead for us."

She shifted and raised her sleeve to wipe her eyes. "We drove for hours and did not stop until late evening. When the truck came to rest, we were all numb from sitting on the metal floorboard and sore from hours of jostling. The senior cadre officer who had ridden in the cab of the truck with the driver shouted at us., 'This is your new home. Get out of the truck and get moving; there's work to be done!'"

The first night, we carried water from a creek that ran at the base of the hill where our sleeping quarters had recently been built. We filled the reservoir of the camp commander's dwelling first, then the cadre barracks and then ours. It took hours to do a bucketful at a time. My mother had stopped crying, as we worked until she saw my hands. It had not taken long for blisters to form and then for them to burst to leave me with bloody flaps of skin on my palms. Hers were the same, but she cried over mine."

Chau had been sitting next to Tuan, both of them across from Lan, and she shifted to face her. She had grown up in small villages and was accustom to the hard manual labor of country living and was not moved. She glared at Lan. "You had an easy life in the cities. Isn't it fair to now have to do your share of the work that benefits the entire country?"

"Chau, is it right to take property that you haven't worked for and are not entitled to from its proper owners?" Tuan shook his head. "What's been done to so many since the war ended, is not fair. It does not create unity. It does not bring the people of Vietnam together."

Chau stiffened as if Tuan had lashed out at her, then stood and walked away without another word.

After a moment Lan quietly commented, "she does not like me."

"She does not understand…" Tuan was studying Chau, who was at the edge of the cleared area—their camp for the night—her arms wrapped tightly around her as she stared into a thick growth of briars and trees that surrounded them. "What the Communists, the cadre, have taught her conflicts with what her eyes have seen and that's confusing."

Lan was young but mature beyond her years. She had seen how Chau looked at Tuan. It was clear she loved him. "She does not like me," and she knew exactly why.

Scott had seen the same thing and agreed with Lan. He would need to talk to Tuan privately though about his concerns regarding Chau. "So you were faced with work, hard labor, you had never done before…"

His voice made Lan look at him as she listened to Tuan translate.

"Yes. We had to clear the land for a large garden, seed it and irrigate daily by carrying buckets of water from the creek. We were told if you want food to eat you will have to work for it." She looked down at her hands resting in her lap.

Scott had noticed her long fingers and how finely formed her hands must have once been. That made him think of Mai playing piano for him so long ago—her soft delicate hands—and how such daily backbreaking manual labor would have ruined their gracefulness, as well. "And then they came to take you from your mother." He prompted her.

The eyes that rose to look at him were rimmed with tears. "Yes." She nodded. "The man who had shown up at our house that first time to tell us we were being moved. The one whose eyes bothered me the way they crawled over me. One evening, when I came in from the field, he was there waiting for me. Two men were with him. They had my mother—one on each side holding her by her arms—as she pleaded with the man, 'please, do not take her' she cried. Not thinking, I tried to go to her and to make the men let her go. The man stepped forward, between us, and put his hand on my chest. Within a moment it went from intending to stop me to his fingers stroking my breasts. He leaned closer, and I felt his breath on my cheek as he said, 'you're coming with me... fight and your mother dies. And you will still go with me.' I stood still. With a final squeeze, his hand dropped from my breast. He laughed over his shoulder toward my mother, 'she is so beautiful,' he told her. That night he took me to the New Economic Zone that he had been made commander of."

CHAPTER 30

NORTH AND EAST OF HO CHI MINH CITY
(FORMERLY SAIGON)

Since they had turned east and then south from Long Khanh, the number of troops did seem fewer. They traveled through the countryside trying to stay parallel and guide themselves, by the road that ran almost directly south toward the coast. About 30 miles south of Long Khanh and 40 miles east of Ho Chi Minh City the number of troops began to increase. Patrols, two to four men in each Jeep, now periodically traveled the highway both north and south and they could see where some were taking side roads to scour the countryside. Either the search was still on for escapees from Suoi Mau, or this was standard cadre procedure to catch refugees headed to the coast.

Seeing the activity on and near the highways and roads, they moved toward the forested areas and had found a stream that seemed to have a southeasterly course. They followed it through miles of a heavily wooded area. In a cluster of fallen trees, they stopped for the night. The next morning, Lan had gone to fill their canteens at the stream when they heard shouting and then her scream.

Even through the stress of hiding and the ever present danger of being captured, Scott had grown stronger from the exercise and all the walking. And the food they'd been able to forage was still more than what Scott and Tuan had eaten in the camp on a daily basis. He was on his feet almost as quickly as Tuan. Chau remained seated. It had become increasingly apparent that she did not care for Lan and wasn't the least bit concerned at hearing her scream.

Tuan reached the point downstream where they had filled canteens the night before with Scott right behind him.

Scott saw the two cadre soldiers first. "Get down!" He grabbed Tuan and pulled him to the ground behind a thicket of bushes and spreading undergrowth. They peeked up over the edge of the brush and could see Lan running up the slope on the far side of the stream away from the two men.

"We have to go after her!" Tuan exclaimed about to rise to his feet again.

Scott held onto his arm and kept him behind the bushes. "She's moving faster than them so she'll get away. If we go chasing after her, making noise, they're going to turn back on us or doing that is gonna get the attention of any other patrols in these woods and then we are in big trouble. She knows by now to get clear and then circle back around."

"Do you think she will?" Tuan settled back on his heels.

Scott was watching as the two men finally made it up the slope from the streambed and moved out of sight over the rise of the hill. He turned to Tuan. "She seems like a smart girl. I think so. Right now, I believe we need to get back to Chau." Scott had his doubts about her, and they had grown even stronger as he watched her glaring at Lan each time they stopped to rest and eat.

They returned to their hiding place to see that Chau had gathered her and Tuan's things. Scott noticed that his and Lan's had been cast to one side.

"We must go now!" She slipped her small pack over her shoulders and handed a slightly larger one to Tuan.

He looked at it, then at her without speaking. Behind her, Scott had picked up his backpack and Lan's. His and Tuan's eyes met over Chau's shoulder. Scott raised his eyebrows, shook his head and shifted his stern look meaningfully at Chau's back.

Tuan took his pack from her and set it on the ground. "No. We are not going anywhere." He sat down beside it and, nodding his agreement, Scott joined him sitting stiffly and awkwardly cross-legged on the ground.

"Are you crazy?" She looked at Tuan and then cast a quick dismissive glance at Scott. "Why?"

Tuan's face was unyielding. "We're going to wait and give Lan time to make it back."

"We must leave her!" Chau had a look of disbelief on her face. "You said that we would be together. I understand about him—that we need to bring him with us," she jabbed a finger at Scott, "there are reasons you felt the need to save him. But why her?"

"You don't understand. We are together. But that now includes Lan. We are not going to abandon a young girl." Tuan turned his head to explain to Scott what he had just told her.

She slung her pack to the ground and squatted on her heels glaring at Tuan. "What if more soldiers come?"

"Then we will have to leave. And maybe even if they don't show up, but it's been too long to continue to wait... maybe then we will have to move on without Lan. But for now, we are going to hold for a couple of hours to give her time to lose those soldiers and make it back here."

* * *

It had been four hours and Lan still had not shown up.

"It has been long enough." Chau was on her feet with her backpack on.

Tuan looked at Scott. "We can't wait any longer... I hate to do it, but we must go."

"If she was able to lose them then she should be back by now," Scott nodded, stiffly rising to his feet.

Chau ignored Scott and went to stand in front of Tuan looking up at him. "We must move fast," she darted a glance at Scott. "He must keep up with us."

Tuan shook his head at her but didn't say anything. He slung his backpack over his shoulder and headed for the path they had found earlier moving them closer in the direction they needed to go to find a boat.

An hour later, they paused at the edge of where the trail cut across a wide dirt road that bisected the woods. It headed toward the fields around the village that they had bypassed. They were about to cross to the other side to continue on the path when they heard the sound of an engine approaching.

"Down!" Tuan cried and then rolled flat in the high grass that bordered the road. Scott was closest to it and in a whisper called back to Tuan.

"It's a Jeep with two men..." he paused then his voice pitched up with excitement. "And a girl!"

As the Jeep passed where they lay, they saw the girl in the back seat with her hands tied behind her. It was Lan. They watched as she cried out when the Jeep hit a hole in the road and threw her to one side and nearly out of the back. The driver slowed, pulled to the far side of the road and stopped. He got out to reposition Lan more securely.

Scott heard Chau's low exclamation. "No!" He saw Tuan rise from the ground and bring his pistol up to aim at the men. Scott got to his knees only to throw himself back down as he heard the crack of a shot and then another. Tuan spun around blood pouring from his thigh. He raised his gun, aimed and fired then shifted and shot again. Scott rolled and came to rest on the road. He scrambled to his feet to see the two soldiers either dead or unconscious beside the Jeep and Lan crying in the back. He looked up and down the road to make sure no one else was around. Glancing over his shoulder, he saw Chau helping Tuan get to his feet and they staggered onto the path toward the Jeep.

"We have to push the Jeep off the road and drag these men into the woods." Tuan gasped.

Scott got into the Jeep and kicked it into neutral. "Lan! Lan, you have to help us." He took a knife out and cut the rope binding her wrists. "Help me push it off the road." They got it rolling, and he felt it pick up speed. Looking over his shoulder, he saw that Tuan was pushing as well, but blood was pumping from his left thigh in a steady stream. They got it deep into the high brush where it couldn't be seen. He looked back, and Chau had already dragged one of the men halfway there as well. Tuan fell to the ground next to the Jeep while

Scott went back and dragged the other dead soldier into the bush underneath a tree.

"Why don't we take the Jeep?" Chau was breathing heavily.

Scott gave her a disbelieving look. "Driving on the roads and highways is a sure way to get caught."

Chau ignored him. She was at Tuan's side checking his wound. Lan looked on, still shaking.

Tuan grimaced as Chau plugged the bullet holes with some moss and strapped it tight with a piece of cloth torn from one of the dead soldier's undershirt. "Let's get going. We need to get as far from here as we can and find someplace to rest for a couple days. But first, strip the men of anything we can use."

Scott felt Chau's icy look at him then saw her give Lan the same glare as she bent over the men going through their pockets. He returned Chau's stony stare. "Let's get going." He bent and lifted Tuan to get underneath one shoulder. They moved him about 100 yards from the Jeep and the bodies of the dead soldiers.

Scott bent stiffly to check Tuan's wounds. Picking the moss from them, he could see that the two bullets had gone through just above the muscle of his thigh, three inches below his crotch, at an angle so that the exit wounds were on the inside of the thigh.

"I don't know how they missed your other leg or your balls. I guess if the leg had not been ahead—forward—of the other, it would be much worse." Scott shook his head as he wadded up a piece of t-shirt torn from one of the dead guards and pressed it against the two ragged exit holes so close together they were almost a single wound.

Chau held another scrap tightly against the entry wounds and began to wind long narrow strips around Tuan's leg to hold them in place.

Tuan tried to sit up and stopped when Scott put his hand flat on his chest. "Lay back! You're bleeding badly, the bullets might've nicked an artery. Moving now could tear it wide open. We need to keep the pressure on these to slow, and hopefully, stop, the bleeding and let it coagulate."

"We can't stay here—even if we're off the road—patrols are going to look for those two." Tuan gestured back in the direction of where they had hidden the bodies. "When they don't check in."

"Shit... I know... I know," Scott cursed softly. "But we can't carry you very far."

"Leave me here then." Tuan grabbed Scott's arm. "I can't walk and can't be moved far even if you carry me." He turned to Chau and repeated what he had just said. "Leave me."

"No!" Scott and Chau both shook their heads. "We'll figure something out." Scott wiped his hands on a scrap piece of cloth, racking his mind about what to do.

Tuan tried to sit up again, and a stab of pain stopped him. "It's already full daylight, we will be spotted and checked out. Then you and I will die and who knows what will happen to Chau and Lan."

Hearing her name, Lan came closer and leaned down to Chau. She told her something but was ignored. Lan moved to Tuan's side, avoiding Chau's glare. She bent down and said something to him.

Tuan looked at her then up at Scott. "She thinks she may know of a place to hide." He quizzed her for a few minutes and shifted to raise on his elbows. "The two soldiers caught her when she fell through an opening into the ground. She couldn't see far into it apparently, but she thinks it opened into a large room underground."

"A tunnel?" Scott asked Tuan.

"It must be that or a bunker complex." Tuan nodded. "There's countless miles of them all over this area."

"Well, then that's our only chance and definitely worth checking out." He looked at Lan. "How far is it from here?" He reached down to make sure the bandages were still secure around Tuan's leg.

"Lan says it's maybe one click, a kilometer or so. She can find it from the road where they dragged her through the brush and briars." Tuan smiled up at Lan, who gave him a shy smile in return. "There might be some supplies—something to help stop the bleeding."

Scott looked from them to Chau, who had been watching and listening intently. He could see by the set of her jaw that her teeth were clenched as she looked at Lan. "I hope so because moving's going to cause you to lose a lot of blood." He shook his head as he looked back down at Tuan. One problem at a time. "Ask Chau to take off her belt. We need it for a tourniquet."

Chau complied but ignored Lan when she reached for it, instead handing it directly to Tuan. He wrapped it above the wound, cinching it tight where his upper leg and crotch met. "We'll have to loosen every minute or so but it should slow my blood loss while we get there." He motioned for Scott and Lan to help him stand. Chau moved forward, forcing Lan to step back.

Two minutes later, Scott under one of Tuan's arms and Chau under the other, they cautiously stepped onto the road.

"I pray to God we don't meet anyone." Scott breathed thinking he'd said it only to himself.

"Amen, brother," Tuan grunted with pain.

Ten minutes later, the tourniquet loosened, blood soaked through the crude bandage. Tuan's right hand periodically dropped to wipe and smear it into the pants leg below the opening they had cut to bandage the wound. He hoped that he was not leaving a trail of blood drops in the dirt that could be followed.

A few steps ahead of them, Lan led the way with a taut, tense, face that flashed its sheen of sweat as she looked over her shoulder every dozen feet to check on them.

***

An hour later, by the dead soldier's watch, Lan stopped and studied the side of the road. "It was right here." She pointed at a trampled area and to two furrows, dug by her feet as they pulled her along, in the soft dirt of the road's edge. "This is where they dragged me onto the road." She pointed to a widened spot just ahead where another, smaller, road bisected the one they were on. "Their Jeep was right there." She stepped off the road and looked up the slope that was the rise of a high hill. "Up there is where I fell and caught my leg. I made too much noise trying to free it." She walked up the slope, which quickly steepened." The two men heard me and then spotted where I was." Lan turned to look back at them. "That's how they caught me."

Tuan was white faced with pain and blood loss. Chau was breathing heavily and Scott even more so. He gasped for air and felt a deep arthritic ache in his legs and shoulders. Lan came back down to his side looking up at the tall, though stooped, American. She said something to him.

"She wants to know if you can make it—if you can make it while helping carry me?" Tuan's face was drawn tight.

Scott raised his head and looked up the hill then at her as she said something else to Tuan.

"She says she can help."

Scott nodded and smiled at her and got a tremulous one in return. "Well, I need her help. Let's get up there and see what we find."

CHAPTER 31

EAST OF HO CHI MINH CITY (FORMERLY SAIGON)

Where Lan had fallen turned out to be a spider hole that was actually the entrance to an extensive series of underground rooms within the hill. A large tunnel ran from the lowest room, for some distance they could not determine, and appeared to parallel the road.

"This is much better." Tuan's gasp was of relief but still tinged with pain as they laid him on a blanket in one corner of the room immediately beneath the access hole. With another grunt of pain, he raised his upper body on his elbows and looked up at him. "All of you," Tuan looked at Scott and repeated it through gritted teeth in Vietnamese for Chau and Lan, "search every room and find any other way in or out."

* * *

Scott recognized the type of the two packs immediately. "Tuan," he called over his shoulder toward the main room at the foot of the spider hole's access ladder. Chau had not left Tuan's side, leaving the search for anything of value to Scott and Lan. They had split up and, in a small room off to the right, he had found medical supplies. He stiffly bent, picked them up and carried to where Tuan laid on a rough pallet Chau had made for him from moldy blankets and the piece of canvas they had scrounged. "These are Navy corpsman field packs." He set them down, carefully knelt and opened them. "Bandages, sulfa powder..." He lined up the contents next to Tuan's leg. "And morphine syrette's." He held one up without puncturing the seal." Do you need it?"

Though white faced with pain and blood loss, Tuan shook his head. "Not until we're sure this place is secure." He scanned the room, checking the openings leading other areas and a passageway that seemed to lead deeper into the bunker. He pointed at the two packs. "Whoever those belonged to, the poor guy must've been new; all the corpsmen I saw in the field carried their supplies in combat engineer packs. They didn't want to be more of a target." He shook his head again and closed his eyes.

"This is going to hurt." Scott stripped off the bloodied rags they had used—pulling the wads packed in the wound used as a plug—and carefully wiped the entry holes. Then dusted them with sulfa powder. "Chau, help me turn him on his side." Tuan translated and, with a grunt, rolled over so Scott could treat the exit wounds the same way. Minutes later, Scott had wrapped them, around his upper thigh, with a compression bandage and then loosened the tourniquet.

***

"How are you feeling?"

Tuan opened his eyes and tried to focus, vaguely remembering Scott had stuck him with a morphine syrette once everything was cleaned and bandaged. He smiled dopily at Lan. "I'm much better..." His eyes half-closed wanting to return to his dream. "Thank you," she put her hand on his shoulder, but he had faded back into sleep.

"Leave him alone," Chau squatted next to Tuan, forcing Lan to move or be knocked over. She took his limp hand. "I'll take care of him."

Lan looked at Scott, and he motioned for her to come sit by him as he opened the combat rations they had found along with three 5-gallon cans that proved to hold water. As he opened tins of meat and beans with a P-38 can opener, he studied Chau and noted the sadness on Lan's face. He wiped his eyes with the back of his hand but managed a smile for Lan. Staying here long enough for Tuan to heal to the point where he could travel was going to be difficult.

CHAPTER 32

LATE JANUARY 1979
SOUTHEAST OF HO CHI MINH CITY

Tuan's wounds had closed, but they still moved slowly toward the coast. They had left the one place where they had been able to hide and rest for more than one day since their escape from the camps. The food from the bunker was exhausted so they were back to foraging and scavenging what they could. Lan had returned from a nearby village with a bag of rice and corn that she had bartered for using the two dead soldiers' watches. She knew better than to hand it to Chau, thinking that she would then prepare a meal for all of them—her focus was solely on herself and Tuan. Scott took it from her, set it aside, and put a pot of water on the open fire to bring it to a boil.

    Lan knelt next to Tuan, ignoring Chau's scowl. "I heard someone in the village talking about their cousins in Bien Chau. They were thinking about moving there since it seems like there are fewer cadre and soldiers in that area. It's also a small fishing village where there will be more food. Maybe that's where we should head. There would be boats there."

"And patrols up and down the coast, watching for people trying to find a boat." Chau's laugh was full of scorn.

Tuan seemed better and stronger. He was sitting up straight and smiled at Lan. "Well," he looked around at each of them, "I'll be able to travel faster soon, and we need to pick a destination." He caught the flash of anger on Chau's face and turned to her. He knew that he and Scott owed getting out of the camp to her and had continually tried to make her feel better about her decision. "Chau, we have to decide." He patted her hand, and that seemed to calm her, but such attention seemed not to last long anymore. "The only way out for us is on a boat. So somewhere on the coast is where we need to head. This village," he gestured at Lan, "is as good a place as any." He understood what the looks on their face meant. "And when we get there, we'll find out if this is the right decision."

CHAPTER 33

End of January 1979

It was nearly thirty miles to Bien Chau and would be a hard march on all of them, especially Tuan. They stayed clear of the main highways and occasionally found paths and trails that ran parallel to them that weren't in too bad of shape as they made their way south.

"What's going on with them?" Scott was walking alongside Tuan matching his slightly slower pace than the two women. He pointed at Chau and Lan, who were striding along almost elbow to elbow ahead of them.

Tuan shrugged and grimaced. Even though the wound was semi-healed, it was still fresh, and after a while, each step sent a stinging pain through his wounded leg. He hoped that it would not tear open, but they could not slow down. "Maybe they're becoming friends." He sounded hopeful at that thought.

"That would be a good thing." Scott hadn't said anything to Tuan, but he still had misgivings about

Chau. She had become increasingly tense and at times had a wild look in her eyes, especially whenever they came across soldiers or officials they had bypassed when they were closer to or on the road. Each time he thought, she's going to shout to them, "he's an American... an American!" And then she would knock his conical hat off to reveal a hated enemy of the people and take credit for capturing the three escapees.

"Yes. Let's hope so." Tuan sensed that Scott had something else to say but had decided not to share it.

* * *

A MANGROVE SWAMP AND FORESTED AREA NEAR THE SOUTHERN COAST

They had stopped at the northeastern edge of a zone that Tuan vaguely recalled from training with the U.S. Marines. It was an enormous wetlands and jungle area that started miles inland and reached all the way to the coast. They were west and just north of Bien Chau, maybe a day's hike to get there. He rubbed his leg and noted the spots of blood where the bullet holes had healed but were beginning to split at the puckered flesh. He would need to bind tighter the bandage he still wore and hoped that it would hold.

Chau looked at Lan. Everything had changed with Tuan once she had joined them. But he didn't see it that way. She shook her head at the thought and wondered, for the hundredth time or more, if Tuan would love her again if Lan were gone. That he had never said that he loved her didn't matter because she knew inside that he must. She glanced at the American and wished that she had never laid eyes on him. Whether or not he would be their access to easily resettling in the United States or not, didn't matter. She could rationalize helping Tuan, after all, he was just a misguided fellow countryman who had followed a corrupt regime and government. Surely re-education would've worked. She had been foolish to help them escape, but she had been caught up in her emotions and love for Tuan. But, her eyes passed over Scott again, in part, she blamed all Americans for what had happened in her country.

* * *

THE NEXT DAY

It had been a hard march but at sunset they reached the outskirts of Bien Chau. They circled around to its southern side, thinking that area was where the fishermen and people with boats would likely be. At the edge of the coastline, they followed it north and within a few miles they discovered a small cove framed on either end by a dense copse of ancient mangroves. They formed a curtain that would have hidden the cove from the coastal waters, until coming right up on it, if it was approached from any direction other than due west from seaward. And they likely would've missed it too, if they hadn't heard the sound of metal on metal and a man cursing. Instead, they would have followed the trail that went inland and pushed through the trees and undergrowth to arc around to a point on the waterfront further north bypassing this secluded cove.

"Do you see him?" Tuan pointed so that Scott could follow along the line of his arm and extended index finger.

Scott nodded. "I do now, but I wouldn't have been able to if you hadn't pointed him out even with the sounds he's making."

Though there was no way for the old man to hear them, he suddenly jerked his head up and looked around. Alarmed that he had unconsciously made so much noise, he needed to check to make sure no one was around him. He picked up his hammer, and the object he had been striking with it and moved away from the square, flat-topped, stone. He walked toward a large clump, a mound twice his height, of trees and foliage that grew from the edge of the water back into a tangled morass of jungle growth.

Scott and Tuan moved closer, careful to not make any noise to startle him. The man stopped and looked around again, was reassured and seemingly thinking no one was around to see him, he set the hammer and metal object he had been holding at his feet. He reached in front of him and grabbed a section of what seemed like a wall of bamboo and greenery. The old man, his arms still corded with muscle, lifted the camouflaged panel and set it to one side. Tuan and Scott crept closer once the man had stepped into the opening of the enclosure he had just revealed. Inside they saw the strike of a match and then a lanterns glow. In that arc of light, they saw the stern of a large fishing boat with the stem of where it's driveshaft and propeller had been exposed. They watched as the old man stood there, looking at the boat, shaking his head.

Taking a deep breath, Tuan stepped into the small clearing. "Hello." As the old man whirled, he held both hands up palms out. "I'm not armed." He saw the man's eyes widen and knew Scott must have followed him.

"Who are you and what is that American doing here with you!"

CHAPTER 34

A Cove Near Bien Chau

Tuan turned to Scott. Lan was directly behind him and behind her was Chau. "The old man, Phan Vu, says his son was a mechanic who kept the engine running." The old man shrugged and looked at them. "He says, but he's just a fisherman. He doesn't trust engines and knows very little about them." Tuan had to smile at the scornful glances the man kept giving the partially disassembled engine. "And that this is the only boat around large enough to take him and his family." The man continued. "He says, he heard that the Communists plan to take over the fishing communities, and this is no longer his, or his family's, country. They must leave."

Scott nodded as he bent to look at the engine. "How many are there in his family?"

Tuan asked and stopped the man long enough to reply to Scott. "12, mostly children."

"With us, that makes sixteen people. He thinks this..." He waved a hand at the length of the dilapidated hull, "will carry all of us?" He had walked around it, and it seemed sound and reliable, but he had doubts.

Tuan had grown up in Saigon and knew nothing about boats. He said something to Phan Vu, who replied and then both men shrugged their shoulders. "Maybe, but if we can't repair the engine, it will not carry anyone. He does not know what to do."

Scott awkwardly bent further, it was difficult since he had little flexibility in his neck, to stick his head into the engine compartment. "It's much bigger than the motorcycle engines I've worked on and rebuilt. But an engine is an engine. Ask him if his son knew what was wrong with it... what needed to be repaired or replaced."

Tuan asked the man who rattled on and then grew quiet. "He says it was the fuel pump and shaft bearings."

Scott straightened, massaging his neck to try and loosen the tight scar tissue of the muscles. "There's more parts off the engine than just that." He scanned the nearby table, trying to identify what was what. "But I think everything is here except the fuel pump and bearings." Scott looked at Tuan. "Does he know where we can find them?"

"Phan Vu says his son never came back from his search for the parts. He stepped on a landmine and two villagers brought part of him home to be buried. They were unable to find his legs, though."

The old man started talking again, and Scott could see the tears in his eyes. "No man should be buried without his legs." Tuan translated. Phan Vu wiped his eyes with the back of a grease smeared hand. "He says there is an engine shop at an old French estate up the coast. That's where his son was going to look for the parts."

"How does he know about it… the engine shop?" Scott asked.

Tuan turned to the old man, asked him then turned back to Scott. "He says, that's where they stole this boat years ago."

* * *

"The old man said his son was killed in an unmarked minefield!" Chau gripped Tuan's arm. "It's too dangerous. You can't do this!" She looked to see if anyone was near. Scott was on the boat peering into the engine compartment, and Lan was beside him holding a flashlight and shining it on the engine for him. "We should leave them—all of them—this is crazy!" She gave his arm a firmer tug that he resisted looking at her until she let go of him.

Tuan bent to pick up his pack, making sure the Lensatic field compass they had found in the bunker was still inside and that his canteen was full. Phan Vu had said it was eight miles to the old French estate and that the road to it had been destroyed long ago. It was now so thickly overgrown that it merged with the jungle and would be a tough hike there and back. Sitting with the old man, he had sketched a crude map of the area and route to the abandoned estate. He looked down at Chau. "I know where his son's body was found, and I'll be careful." He settled his pack on his shoulders and though he felt far from it, he smiled at her. "Help Scott in any way that you can while I'm gone."

"What if you don't come back?" She clung to his arm again.

Tuan looked over at Scott and Lan and knew that they would not make it alone. Not without him. Not with Chau. He gently took her hand from his arm and then touched her shoulder. She closed her eyes as he told her, "I'll be back. We're all going to get out of here."

Chau didn't open them until he had left. When she did, she looked directly at Lan, who was still with Scott. She knew exactly what she was going to do.

CHAPTER 35

NEAR THE FRENCH ESTATE

Two miles behind Tuan was the spot where Phan Vu's son had died. The machete he had given him was old. The blades width had been thinned by decades of sharpening, but it sliced easily through thick vines, creepers, and small branches. Tuan wiped his eyes and caught his breath, and thought about Phan Vu's son, dying torn apart by a landmine that had ripped him in half. He would likely have died similarly if it weren't for his training and experience. Someone—crazy with paranoia or just plain stupid—had mined not only the once clear route to the old French estate; they had also set mines in and among the trees and brush line off the path and road. Thankfully, most of them had been hurriedly planted and showed still clear signs, mounds, that an experienced eye could tell was a landmine.

Yet, not trusting what he couldn't see, he still stepped on stumps, sections of and in some cases entire fallen trees and stones to stay off the ground as much as possible. Even so, just minutes ago he had found himself stuck in the middle of several mines clustered for 10 feet in every direction except for the way he had just come that he had hacked through the densest underbrush encountered so far. To go forward, he had jumped to grab the thick vines overhead and swung from one to another until clear. With each pull and swing, he had prayed it would not give way and land him on what he was trying to avoid.

He was now even more exhausted but still smiled at the childhood memory of his father taking him to see an American Tarzan movie when he was a young boy. He lost the pleasure of it as he breathed deep and could almost taste the smell of rotting vegetation and of some animal that must've died nearby. His arms felt like lead, but he raised the machete and chopped down into the thick mass in front of him.

Clang! The sound and shudder of metal striking metal ran through his arm and startled him. He nearly dropped the machete. Getting a firmer grip and using it as a poker, he prodded straight out from him. A softer metallic sound came from beneath the vines and foliage. Dropping the machete to hang from the strap around his wrist, he gripped handfuls and pulled, using his weight as much as his remaining strength. Large patches torn away he could now see what he had hit. A row of wrought-iron bars, about eight-feet high, with cross pieces every two feet. He felt his way along them and in a dozen feet felt the rough texture of a concrete pillar. He had found the main entrance to the estate.

CHAPTER 36

THE COVE NEAR BIEN CHAU

Chau saw Lan sitting alone near the campsite where they had stored their few possessions once Tuan came to an agreement with the old man to help repair the boat in exchange for passage. He had sold the old man, as he had her, on the immense benefit of having an American with them whenever they arrived at the refugee camp. Scott, once he had communication with authorities would get immediate attention and he, in turn, could help them. Among tens of thousands of refugees, something like that could make all the difference in their treatment. So Scott would make it onto the boat.

She approached Lan. "Where is Scott?"

Lan looked up, surprised that Chau was talking to her. The past few days she had seemed more friendly toward her, but Lan suspected that it wasn't sincere as much it was to put Tuan at ease. "He is with the Phan Vu and his youngest son. At the boat."

"Come with me." Chau reached out a hand toward Lan and beckoned her away from the cleared area of the campsite. "There's something I want to show you that maybe we should take with us on the boat."

"Tuan should be back soon." Lan hesitated, not getting up.

Chau stepped forward into the light from the fire and smiled down at Lan. "I think it is something that will help us. Who knows how long we will be on the boat. But I need help to carry it." She gestured again with her hand for Lan to stand and come with her.

"Okay," Lan still seemed reluctant. "I'll help you."

Carrying an old, lighted, kerosene lantern, Chau moved away from the encampment to where the ground became increasingly spongy, and she could feel her feet sink slowly into it with each step. After about five minutes' walk, she turned around. She set the lantern on a waist high stump. It cast enough light for both of them to see each other. From underneath her short jacket, she drew out a pistol. Its barrel had an oiled, blue, gleam in the lantern light. "Don't move and don't make a sound." She brought the pistol up and leveled it at Lan's face.

"What are you doing, Chau?" Lan was scared but kept her voice steady and low.

"I'm taking care of a problem. We don't need you."

Lan took a half step back and stopped when Chau quickly moved closer and tightened her grip on the pistol. "Why do you hate me... I've done nothing to you."

"I've seen how you look at Tuan." Chau's face contorted into a snarl, "And he's mine. He and I will be together whether that's here or in America."

Lan's face paled even further. "I've never told Tuan that I love him."

"Bitch. I see it in your eyes. I hear it in the way you talk to him." Chau shuddered and gritted her teeth. "You can't have him; only I will..."

Lan was close enough to see her finger tighten on the trigger. She heard splashing and heavy breathing to their left and turned to face it at the same time as Chau.

"What are you two doing out here?" Tuan was breathing heavily and covered in mud and green moss. He looked from Lan to Chau and then saw the gun in her hand. "What are you doing Chau... Put that away."

She had lowered the handgun as Tuan talked but took two steps closer to Lan and raised it to level with her chest. "She's not going with u--" she started to pull the trigger.

Tuan threw the wrench he been holding, and it struck Chau's hand making her drop the pistol. "Stop this, Chau." He put himself between her and Lan. "Listen, there are patrols, squads of cadre approaching Bien Chau. I don't know why they're here, but we only have a few hours before they blanket the area. I had to cut through the swamp to avoid them," he stepped closer. "Chau," he stooped to pick up the pistol, "whatever you're thinking you were going to do, stop it. There's nothing between Lan and me--" He turned to look at her and get her acknowledgment that was true.

Lan did the worst thing she could have... she rushed to him, threw her arms around his neck and held him tight. Over her shoulder, Tuan saw Chau's stark, white, furious face just before she turned and ran. He knew that if she made it through the swamp, she would cross one of the roads and eventually come to one of the patrols. In her rage, she would turn them in. He stuck her pistol in his belt and picked up the lantern.

"What are we going to do?" Lan cried.

Tuan raised a hand, carrying a bag that clanked as pieces shifted around. "I got the parts that Scott needs. We're going to fix the boat and get out of Vietnam." He grabbed her hand and pulled her along as he raced to where the boat was hidden and Scott and the old man were working.

* * *

Scott didn't even turn away from repacking the old bearings when Lan ran toward them and breathlessly reported to Tuan who was on the boat, cleaning vines and foliage from the deck "What's she saying... did she find Phan Vu and tell him to hurry?"

"She says twelve men, maybe more, are in the village questioning people. She described them, and they sound like a mix of cadre camp guards and regular soldiers." Tuan stopped Lan and barked a question at her. Tight-faced and frightened she looked at Scott, nodded and then answered him. "Shit!" Tuan tugged at Scott's elbow.

"I can only go so fast, I'm so--" the tugging was insistent, and he brusquely turned to face Tuan, who had him by the elbow. "What!"

"Lan says that the officer leading the men... he's asking the villagers if they have seen an American with a badly scarred face. They are spreading out to cover the area in their search."

Scott recoiled; it couldn't be him. There was no way it could be him. He wiped his face leaving green-black bearing grease in the carved grooves that his regrown beard barely covered. "It doesn't matter. I gotta get the shaft back in and then we have to roll this..." he slapped the hull, "into the water." He looked around. "Where's the old man?"

"Lan says she found him gathering his family, food, and water." Tuan looked at the old pocket watch the man had given him. "He said they'd be here in an hour."

Scott wiped his eyes with a clean corner of the cloth rag he held in one hand. "How long ago was that?"

"About 30 to 40 minutes ago," Tuan replied. He looked at the bench, and the scattering of bits and pieces of components was almost all gone. Scott had been working feverishly, and he prayed that it all had gone back together correctly, and the engine would start. "He should be back in 20 minutes."

Scott nodded. "I'll be ready to test the engine by then."

They looked at each other. If the engine did not fire up, they knew they would likely be captured before the day was over.

CHAPTER 37

February 1, 1979
The Cove near Bien Chau

Scott was positioned over the engine and motioned at the old man to try the ignition. The motor made that lug lug, chuff, and churning, sound of an old tired, cold, engine that just did not want to turn over. He worried that the battery wouldn't last long enough to kick the engine into starting. He primed it, shooting fuel directly into the cylinders, praying to God he had not flooded it. He motioned to the old man. He saw him punch the ignition button and with a cough and a billowing of blue-gray smoke the engine fired. He flashed a thumbs up at Tuan, who grinned and held Lan, his arm around her shoulders.

As the old man reversed the engine to pull them further off the little beach, Scott saw that Tuan had stopped grinning. Engine sputtering, they managed to pull about 50 feet from the narrow beach. Then it died. The backwash of the surf kept them about the same distance from land, but the tidal change and the current would eventually push them back toward shore. He looked up and gestured back toward the beach.

Scott already had the engine housing off and was peering inside. Tuan was at the stern, eyes scanning the shore. The binoculars he used were old, French made, and had only one cracked lens. He lowered them to wipe his eyes. When he raised them, he spotted her at the same time that her cry carried over the water.

"Tuan, I'm sorry!" She came to the water's edge and stopped.

"Come on," he beckoned to her. "You can make it!" Behind him, he heard the engine cough and almost catch. "Hurry, Chau!"

Scott looked up at Tuan's shout. Next to him Lan straightened, and he felt her tense, her gaze locked on the beach. She too saw Chau, now knee-deep in the surf. She shouted to Tuan and pointed. Two soldiers had entered the clearing and raised their rifles aiming at the boat. Chau wheeled around and ran toward them just as they fired, nearly hitting Tuan.

The engine started with a roar, and Scott felt the boats roll increase, it's beam to the waves. Phan Vu opened the throttle, pulling them away faster and putting the rudder over to keep the bow pointed out to sea. It took a moment for the heavy boat to pick up any speed. They seemed to be barely crawling through the waves.

As the boat turned out to sea, Scott looked over his shoulder and saw that Chau had charged the two men. The men were surprised by her attack and she managed to get the rifle from one, shot him and then the other. More men, two of them carrying a heavy machine gun, flooded into the clearing. She dropped the gun as a man, an officer wearing khakis, approached her with his pistol drawn. The officer said something to her, she replied and then turned to face the boat and screamed.

Tuan and Scott heard her clearly. "Go... Go!" Chau shouted and started to say something else, then lunged at the man. The crack of a single pistol shot carried sharply over the water. Then came the guttural sound of spewing, large-caliber, rounds from the machine gun. Some of them skipped off the water, several slammed in the stern of the boat as it rode higher in the boat, with its nose down into the swell of the trough.

Scott looked over his shoulder and saw more men in uniforms moving through the mangroves. Several of them, struggling through the tangle of undergrowth, carried another heavy machine gun and belts of ammunition. A dozen soldiers were now in the clearing where they had launched the boat. They raised their rifles, but the pitching of the boat on the waves threw their aim off. It was either that or poor marksmanship as bullets struck the thick hull but, other than knocking some chunks of wood from the deck rails, there was no other damage. The swells grew, the boat chugged and pulled itself up them and down their seaward side. After ten minutes running the trough and climbing the shore bound waves, they were adequately screened from the beach.

Tuan slumped to the deck, not looking up for some time, he held his head in his hands. Chau had saved him... saved them, again. For that, he would never forget her.

* * *

After two rough hours of beating against the sea to put more distance between them and the shore, Tuan had conferred with the old man. Based on what they had heard from scraps of radio reports, they set a course for Pulau Galang off the Indonesian coast. The static-filled Voice of America reports and broadcast had said that the island had been opened officially, several months before, as a refugee camp. The report also said boats were arriving daily from Vietnam carrying hundreds, possibly even thousands, of refugees. And those were just the ships that managed to survive the ocean transit. Most were small, overloaded and often attacked by pirates. Thousands of people, including children, had died at sea and never made it to the refugee camp.

By late into that first night on the ocean, they had made their way into the major shipping lanes. The sky was overcast, and it was unbelievably dark. Scott felt the low wind skimming over the surface of the water and with it came a sense of large objects moving in the distance. His eyes focused for several minutes on what he thought was a set of running lights that appeared to be coming near. "Tuan." He shook him awake. "I think a freighter or a tanker is headed this way." Tuan scrambled up, grabbed the lantern and lighted it.

They watched as the ship's lights grew larger and closer and they could see a spreading, deeper, blackness on the water well within eyesight of them. Its aspect changed and now seemed to be running parallel to them and would soon cross its closest point. And if it kept going in that direction it would soon be moving away from them.

"We have to get its attention," Tuan made his way to the bow of the boat, standing as tall as he could while still balancing to ride the pitch and roll of the vessel. He raised the lantern high over his head and began to move it slowly side to side.

Scott had followed him bringing along a square piece of cardboard. "We need to signal so that he'll know we are in distress." He handed Tuan the cardboard.

Tuan lowered the lantern to head height and used the sheet of cardboard to screen and then reveal the light in a signal: SOS SOS SOS. After several minutes, they saw what had to be the bow lights of the ship starting to turn directly toward them. By now the others were all awake and anxiously watching. The bulk of the ship approaching them had slowed and was moving cautiously. Scott expected any minute for a searchlight to stab out and see them. To be sure that the ship understood their dire need Tuan began to signal: R—F—G then a pause and again R—F—G. Within a minute or two they could tell that the ship—a large tanker—was now turning away from them. They watched incredulously as its lights faded in the distance.

"Why would they leave us—why would they turn away and abandon us?" Tuan was mad. Angrier than Scott had ever seen him.

"I'm not sure, but I think when they found out we were a refugee boat they decided to ignore us so that they weren't caught up with what happens if they pick us up. They'd be required to comply with international maritime law that would mean breaking their transit to deliver us to authorities or a local refugee camp." Scott laughed scornfully. "There'd be reports and paperwork to file. It seems they didn't want that kind of hassle. So we're on our own."

CHAPTER 38

They had been at sea for two days. Scott had nothing left in his stomach, but something sure felt solid rising in his throat. He had been on the water a lot as a young man, had surfed for years and had never been this seasick.

He heard the steady chug of the engine change to a spitting, staccato, gasping sound. He watched as Phan Vu, the old man, checked the fuel tank, but he knew he would find there was plenty. He had checked it himself 30 minutes ago.

Phan Vu nodded toward him that there was fuel. As he screwed the cap back on the gas tank, with a final sputter, the engine stopped. The boat's wallowing became even worse since it was unable to make way and ride bow on into the swells.

Scott closed his eyes and again felt chunks come up in his throat. "Dammit!" He swallowed a mixture of bile and saliva as he stood and unsteadily shambled to the engine and lifted the housing off. Equally sick and pale looking, Tuan watched him. Lan sat nearby without the close to puking look that Tuan and Scott had on their face. She hadn't seemed bothered at all by the motion.

"Can you fix it?" Tuan asked.

Scott stumbled and nearly fell, catching himself on the hatch coaming. "I don't know." Thirty minutes later, he knew that it was the gas filter. It was old, full of sediment and years past functioning properly. There was no way to fix it, and they didn't have a replacement. He looked over at Tuan, who had leaned forward to watch him. "The fuel filter is shot." Tuan relayed that information to the others. "There's nothing I can do with it," Tuan told them that as well.

For several minutes, they sat there swaying as the boat rocked from side to side and rose and fell bow to stern. Tuan lifted his head and talked to Phan Vu and then turned to Scott.

"He says we should be only two days from landfall. Getting the engine started, we can stay on course. Without power the current pushes way off and out to sea and further away."

Scott nodded but didn't know what to say. If the engine would not run… they couldn't maintain course.

Tuan put a hand on his shoulder. "Can the engine run without the filter?"

"Yes, but not long without ruining it," Scott said straightening with a thoughtful look in his eye.

Tuan had a similar look. "Could it make it for two more days?"

"I think so!" Scott grinned at him. He shuffled to the engine and with a couple of twists and turns he had detached the filter. He then took the fuel line and connected it directly to the engine, double checking to make sure the fittings were both tight and not leaking. He signaled to Phan Vu, who was now standing at the motor's switch. Scott gave him a thumbs up, and he pressed ignition. The engine stuttered at first as Scott primed it... then it fired up, and they felt the boat settle as Phan Vu notched the throttle up and headed them into the waves.

* * *

FEBRUARY 5, 1979
LANDFALL—TAREMPA

"Scott..."

He tightened his eyes, and in his mind, he could see her waving to him.

"Scott."

She was closer now and in her arms was a little girl. The soft way she said his name; her accent flavored the English, smoothing it into a caress from her lips. Lips that would curve with a smile, one that seemed just for him. He felt her lean toward him; her hand on his shoulder. He knew it would soon come up to tug at his hair. She had always teased him about its sunshine color and length. It was one of the things she found attractive about him. He smiled and closed his eyes tighter.

"Scott!"

Her hand roughly gripped and shook him.

"Scott!"

He opened his eyes. Lan was beside him, kneeling, with her hand on his shoulder. For a second, the overlay of Mai's lovely face hung there—a facade layered over Lan's that teased him with Mai's eyes before it evaporated like mist at sunrise. He struggled to sit up. "What is it, Lan?"

She didn't understand English but knew what he meant. She pointed to Tuan, who was in the bow of the boat with Phan Vu. Over the gasping of the dying engine, he heard the sound of surf breaking on rocks. The boat was rolling with the short, choppy, motion that meant it was in proximity to land. He groaned as Lan helped him stand.

He called louder, this time to Tuan, "What's going on?" Stiff at the knees and hips he shambled to him and looked over his shoulder. It was land and on a narrow strip of beach, what appeared to be a middle-aged man was waving them away. He held an old rifle in one hand as he gestured vigorously with the other. He looked angry.

Tuan turned to Scott. "He doesn't want us to land. He keeps saying, 'Too many... too many.'"

"What do we do? The engine is shot." Scott cocked his thumb toward its housing that vibrated and shook with the rough choking sound of its last gasp. "We're not going anywhere with that thing." He noted that the tide drawing them toward the beach was already weakening. "We're as close as we can get… and soon we'll be pulled out to sea again."

Tuan kicked his sandals off, pulled his shirt over his head and handed it to Scott. "I'm going to talk to him." He stepped to the edge of the boat and slid over the side into the water.

It was 100 feet of rough, choppy, water strewn with rocks. Scott knew Tuan was weak from days of seasickness, no food, and the little water that he had been able to keep down. He watched him struggle to the small area of the beach that wasn't obstructed by rocks.

* * *

Tuan breathed heavily and spat a mouthful of brackish seawater to one side as he stood, got his balance, and then approached the man.

"I told you, go away!" The man was still mad but hadn't raised the rifle that he held firmly in two hands, its barrel angled toward Tuan. "You're too many, too many."

Tuan wiped stinging saltwater from his eyes. "Is this Pulau Galang?"

"No!" His head shook angrily. "No, this is Tarempa."

"We are refugees from--"

The man cut him off. "I know what you are, and it does not matter where you came from."

Tuan raised his hands, pleading with the man. "We don't have any other place to go and no way to get there if we did." Tuan looked at the man who had shifted around Tuan to stare at the boat.

Tuan half turned to look at it too and saw that Phan Vu, his children, and grandchildren now lined the shore side of the boat facing them. With them was Lan and Scott, who stood out. Even bent and bowed, he was still the tallest and his hair in the sun, the brightest.

"Please help us," Tuan asked again. Then he noticed the man was wearing a soldier's utility shirt, frayed and worn, clearly many years old with an Indonesian Army communication specialist's badge. "You're a soldier?"

Seeing what Tuan was looking at, the man touched it with one hand. "I was... a long time ago."

"And when you were done as a soldier, you found a peaceful place... a quiet place." Tuan studied the man's face. "Like this." He gestured inland.

The man met Tuan's gaze. "Yes," he shook his head sadly, "but no longer."

"The war and strife of my country have spilled out," Tuan waved a hand at the boat. "And we have run from it. From those who have stolen our country and oppress and abuse the innocent."

The man's face had relaxed, the deeply etched lines softening. The rifle now hung down at his side, pointing at the ground.

Tuan continued, "I was a soldier too, so I am not so innocent. They…" he gestured at the boat, "are."

The man looked at him. "What about the tall one, that man." He pointed at Scott.

"He is an American, a journalist that was held captive and tortured after the war."

A quick intake of breath whistled through the man's teeth, "The Americans fled your country nearly four years ago!"

"This one didn't make it out." Tuan paused as the man stared again at Scott and the others. "Will you help us—can you help us—get to the refugee camp on Pulau Galang?"

The man shook his head. "There is a small camp here that processes…" he paused, "people like you. I help them with their communications gear. I'll radio them for you. They will come and process you and at some point will transfer you to the larger camp." He shook his head again and sighed. "Go ahead and bring your people ashore."

CHAPTER 39

PULAU GALANG

Once they were in the camp, they heard the stories of others that had been there for a while already. The tens of thousands of refugees crowded on the island lived in makeshift huts two and three stories high made of salvaged timbers from wrecked boats, plastic sheets, tin cans and corrugated iron sheets. The latrines overflowed and rainstorms sent a flood of filthy water through the camp. All food and clean water had to come from the Indonesian mainland. Sanitation was nonexistent, and disease ran wild through the camp.

Without Scott, Tuan knew things would not have gone as well as they had in the refugee camp. His presence had immediately given them access to the highest camp echelon and streamlined his and Lan's blue card processing. But an American prisoner of war escaping Vietnam nearly four years after the war ended would make international news. Scott's story would spread like wildfire if it came out and his picture would, as well. And that was the thing at the heart of the matter. It was what drove Scott from the day they landed to speak privately with only the refugee camp's leader and to swear Tuan and Lan to secrecy. They had also discussed that on the boat with the old man and his family. Once Scott's intervention managed to get them priority processing, they vanished. They had not been seen since and had no doubt quickly merged with the thousands of other refugees. Scott, Tuan, and Lan had stuck together. Tuan had managed the private meeting between Scott and the head of the camp.

"I don't understand." The man looked and sounded tired as well as confused. "With one phone call, I could have a United States Navy helicopter here to pick you up and then you would be headed home." He waited for Scott to reply but he didn't raise his head. "Don't you want to see your family?"

That did make Scott look up. He was cleaner, and his beard was trimmed, but all that had done was reveal how terribly he had been disfigured at Bach's hands. "More than anything..." He reached to swivel the gooseneck lamp on the desk to spotlight his face. His eyes bored into the camp leaders then Tuan's and back. The man looked away; he couldn't meet Scott's glare. "More than anything I want to see them... to see and hold my wife and daughter! But I don't want them to see me like this." He shoved the light from him and lowered his head again into the palms of his hands, elbows on his knees.

The camp leader now understood. "I'm sure they won't care."

Scott snorted at the lie. He had seen the look in the man's eyes only moments before. "But I care. How can I put my wife and daughter through that? Even when the shock lessens and all the whispers and sidelong looks at me are no longer noticed... that reaction will always be there. And there will be some that will pity me. I could probably deal with that." He raised his head to stare at the camp leader. "What would be worse will be knowing that they also will pity my wife and child, and that's how they will act toward them."

Tuan leaned forward and put his hand on his friend's shoulder. When they had escaped—were on the run—and especially that last night and morning on the boat before landfall, he had watched Scott's hands touch and trace the scars on his face and neck. Scott had begun to realize what a successful escape meant. And that his past, what had happened to him, wasn't something he would ever escape. He would always be reminded when he looked into a mirror and in the eyes of those around him.

CHAPTER 40

FEBRUARY 19, 1979
PULAU GALANG

With the promise to keep Scott's name and identity out of it the refugee camp commander, working with the American refugee coordinator, arranged to expedite processing for Tuan and Lan to enter the United States. It wouldn't be long before they left and he'd be alone again. He rubbed his face and knew that was how it had to be. Maybe that would be so for the rest of his life. But there were some things that he had to do until that was resolved, one way or the other.

He had learned through the American refugee coordinator that Jason Kenyon a freelance journalist he had met at the Caravel Hotel in Saigon, was still based in Singapore. He had sent a message to him, at Scott's request, asking him to come to Pulau Galang to meet an important refugee. Refusing to identify who that refugee was—saying only that it was a story for the decade—was sure to make Jason curious enough to come see what it was all about.

* * *

With delays caused by truck and boat breakdowns, it had taken him two days to get to the camp. He had barely caught bits and pieces of news on static-filled radios but knew all Hell was breaking loose on the newswire as he stepped into the refugee camp commander's private office. Jason wondered again what was so pressing about a refugee that the American coordinator would call in a favor owed that would bring him here and now.

He entered the office to see the refugee camp commander and the American coordinator seated around a large metal desk. Another man off to the side, in the shadows, was sitting with his back to the door. They were listening to a radio broadcast. He stood in the doorway riveted by what he was hearing:

China attacks Vietnam!

China, now under Deng Xiaoping, starting economic reform and opening trade with the West, is growing increasingly defiant of the Soviet Union. On November 3, 1978, the Soviet Union and Vietnam signed a twenty-five-year mutual defense treaty, which made Vietnam the linchpin in the Soviet Union's 'drive to contain China.'

On January 1, 1979, Chinese Vice-premier Deng Xiaoping visited the United States for the first time and told American President Jimmy Carter: "The little child is getting naughty, it's time he be spanked."

On February 15, the first day that China could have officially announced the termination of the 1950 Sino-Soviet Treaty of Friendship, Alliance and Mutual Assistance, Deng Xiaoping declared that China planned to conduct a limited attack on Vietnam. The reason cited for the attack was to support China's ally, the Khmer Rouge of Cambodia, in addition to the mistreatment of Vietnam's ethnic Chinese minority and the Vietnamese occupation of the Spratly Islands which were claimed by China.

To prevent Soviet intervention on Vietnam's behalf, Deng warned Moscow the next day that China was prepared for a full-scale war against the Soviet Union. In preparation for this conflict, China put all of its troops along the Sino-Soviet border on an emergency war alert, set up a new military command in Xinjiang, and even evacuated an estimated 300,000 civilians from the Sino-Soviet border. In addition, the bulk of China's active forces (as many as one-and-a-half million troops) were stationed along China's border with the Soviet Union.

The broadcast ended, and Jason knew he should be checking the story with his sources in Singapore and covering this unbelievable news and not here, in the office of a refugee camp commander. He sat down. "Okay, I'm here. Now can you tell me why?"

The unknown man sitting off to the side took his hat off and turned, lifting his face to the light hanging over the camp commander's desk. "I'm the reason you're here, Jason."

The shock on his face was first at the grotesque scars on the man's face, and then he looked beyond them and recognized the man. "Scott! We thought you died in Saigon!"

Scott shook his head. "I've lived a story worth telling but I need your help with something else, and you can't disclose my identity or let it out that I am still alive."

"I don't understand. Why –"

Scott cut him off. "Just sit down and listen. I'll explain everything."

***

Jason had worked out the details with Scott. The plan was for Scott, with the help of the refugee camp commanders and coordinators, to travel throughout Southeast Asia and investigate and write articles on human rights abuse in Thailand, Malaysia, Indonesia and the Philippines. He would have the backing of the United Nations High Commissioner for Refugees who had also agreed to conceal his identity.

Scott would investigate conditions throughout the region and provide information, some of which was to be used to prosecute perpetrators of human rights abuses. Some of it would be turned into series of articles he would send to Jason who would then put them out under his byline and attribute a source in the region whose identity was withheld to protect their safety.

* * *

Four months later Jason Kenyon received the first article from Scott:

Make Love not War

June 1979

Twelve years ago, 1967, in the United States was the Summer of Love. It was a social phenomenon and season that never reached

Vietnam, whose country was mired in a blood-red, Hazy Shade of Winter that continues as I write this. War—not love—has ruled Southeast Asia for decades, if not centuries. It culminated, as a means to an end, on April 30, 1975, with the fall of a democratic South Vietnam.

War is not the opposite of love; not the opponent of love. It is the absence, not the antithesis of love and in that void... hate forms.

Avarice creates the circumstances that in turn creates the conditions that lead—willingly or unwillingly, wittingly or unwittingly—to conflict. For nations, it is usually the leadership cadre that steps onto that slippery slope to war. The public is fed the message that, "wrongs must be righted" or that "national interest must be protected–national security ensured..." And there are times when those are valid reasons—not excuses—to fight. But also, sometimes, the reasons don't stay true; in honest assessment they wither and become excuses for those who use conflict and war—fueling hatred—as a means to an end. To achieve the result that solidifies their power furthers their agenda and benefits them despite all the damage done to those—and what—they purport to lead.

Even the poorest nations now have access to weapons capable of destruction unimagined 100 years ago, when colonialism and imperialism was a global aim, and some countries felt a global right. Their comparative economic and/or military might make right; they could and did enforce their national will on weaker nations. They played at it as if it was a game. Though empires have come undone since the end of World War II, onto that clearing of the chessboard has flowed the covert game of King-making, straw man shell games and puppet governments. And overtly, the age-old era of strongman dictators... all rising on the tide of a self-serving revolution.

To save mankind—to save ourselves—we must realize that we are not just nations and our world—its nations—is not a field of play. All species, human, and animal, share this planet.

We must begin to think of ourselves as stewards and not Masters (or those who wish to become one).

We must learn that we can bring about change—not by revolution—through love, compassion, and understanding. Through sharing global resources and the treasures found within each nation's cultural heritage and taking the good to enrich our global society, we can unite our world with love and not destroy it by war.

A month later he had received:

Going Backward

The history of mankind is a continuous, never-ending struggle for power. Hence, revolutions. Most people think that a revolution is where the just, those in the right, rise and rebel against the unjust, those in the wrong.

A revolution is supposed to be about fighting against what is old—entrenched—and evil. The rebels battle against a—usually corrupt—regime that subjugates its people. Such a government is typically stagnant and focused on maintaining the status quo and its power base.

In recent history, the Communists in Vietnam spread propaganda that now is the time for a proletarian dictatorship and to establish a new world order. And so, the North—the Communists—warred with South Vietnam. Its belief was that their ideology was superior to that of democracy and South

Vietnam. No government is perfect but what the North offered with their revolution was nothing more than party-line propaganda dressed up as an effort to liberate, what they called, their brothers and sisters in the South. Their agenda was pushed forward with increasing aggression and terrorism. Those not willing to subjugate their freedom, democracy, and human rights fought back. In the name of the two conflicting ideologies, people in power mobilized their forces and launched a war.

But their revolution is — was—a facade and nothing but a means to an end. The end of a free society and a devolution—regression—relegating those who fought for or supported the South to imprisonment (leading in countless cases to death) at worst and to serfdom at best.

They—the North—waved their flag over a country they claimed to have unified. But it waves over the blood and bones of thousands of formerly free souls and that of the living who still suffer.

People under the Communists in Eastern Europe are said to be living 'behind an iron curtain.' It's lesser known that most people in the free world are governed and kept 'behind a smoke curtain.' When Nixon campaigned in 1968, he promised to end the Vietnam War with a secret plan. As it unfolded, his strategy was to wheel and deal with China, at the peace accords in Paris, to deliver South Vietnam to the Communists.

Wars are begun within a tangle of lies and betrayals. Political and economic maneuvering is used to twist and turn leaders in small developing countries to carry out the agendas of conflicting superpowers. Regimes founded by, and in some cases still run, by dictators such as Ho Chi Minh, Pol Pot, Kim Il Sung were, and still are supplied with guns and weapons to kill their own people by the very superpowers who lament the region's instability and violence.

These superpowers execute their wars, with total disregard for human lives, lost, through their proxies, resulting in the bloody conflicts and wars that rip countries apart. The superpowers, including the U.S., make deals with devils and bargain with the lives of millions of innocent civilians in these small countries. Sadly, there are always enough dictators, greedily cruel leaders, willing to carry out the superpowers' gambits, because those dictators themselves are hungry for power.

Millions of South Vietnamese, civilian and military, were imprisoned, tortured and murdered. Their blood is on the hands of not only the dictators but also that of the leaders of the superpowers whose machinations brought about the war. After it, those that lived lost their homes, properties, and families. Hundreds of thousands risked their life at sea for freedom. All because of stories and lies that led their country into chaos.

Over the course of the next six months, he received three more articles and then no more. He contacted the coordinator in Pulau Galang who did not know where Scott was but that he had been providing a steady stream of information to the United Nations High Commissioner for Refugees office. But he didn't have any idea if he would send in more articles:

The Pyramid Scheme

The middle level, believing in all that those above them espouse, are what build—but never control—the base of the pyramid. They and those below them have to believe that the party's ideology is the only way—their only path—to a fruitful life.

They have to believe that what they support, is worthy.

But it is not.

The propaganda, the revolution that had been successfully concluded, the re-education of the proud defeated, the New Economic Zone relocation, all serve a particular purpose.

And that purpose is to serve only those at the very top of the pyramid. Where the rulers sit. Where power and the newly redistributed wealth resides. The upper echelon—that inflict but are above the suffering, so far above the abuses of human rights—sit on high and reap the benefits of a system that is not what the people far below them believe it to be.

Communism has repeatedly proven that it is nothing but an illegal means to take the work of many and reward those—the few—at the apex. While those at the bottom, like Atlas in Greek mythology, bear the weight of their world; the mass of lies known as communism.

Uncle Ho's Big Lie

I've written recently about the revolution and how it and communism are not what the Democratic Republic of Vietnam claimed it to be during, and at the end, of the Vietnamese war on April 30, 1975. And the subsequent annexation of South Vietnam to form the current Socialist Republic of Vietnam can all be traced to a man who was the biggest liar of all.

The cult of personality that surrounded him—continuing after his death and up to present day—recasts him as a flawless, unblemished, man and leader. But, in fact, he was deeply flawed and cruel.

In 1953, Ho ordered to 'dau to' (publicly denounce) Nguyen Thi Nam, a woman, to execute her cruelly in public. Nguyen Thi Nam was an affluent woman who had contributed her wealth and social influence to support (provide food and money) during the early days of the Vietnam Communist Party.

She was literally a benefactor to the highest-ranked communists including Ho, Truong Chinh, and Le Duc Tho. They killed her in the name of the proletarian class, but in reality to confiscate all her wealth for the use of the party. Her two sons, both fighting on the Communist's side at the time during their campaign, were discharged from service and imprisoned. This was done to mobilize people for his infamous "land reform" that resulted in the killing of some 200,000.

The legend that Ho chose to live a celibate life, devoting his life for his country, is a lie. Ho was a callous womanizer. He ordered his subordinates to murder one of his young lovers, Nong Thi Xuan, and her two cousins to preserve his facade of a saint-like leader.

Ho, 68 years old that time, was told to stop kissing little schoolgirls during a trip to Indonesia in 1958. He loved to kiss them on the lips whenever he got close to them. Indonesian authorities officially objected his inappropriate and dirty habit.

Yet none of that stopped him from being deified by those who benefited the most from him and by his closest followers for personal and political reasons.

He intentionally chose one line from the U.S. Constitution to include in his 'Declaration of Independence for Vietnam:' that the people have the right to live free and to pursue happiness. He did so to cast his revolution in the proper light; to paint it in the appropriate colors. To hide the fact of the biggest lie. That he was nothing but a demagogue that founded a proletarian dictatorship.

The Climb of Dictators

Revolutions are intended to remove from power those who abuse that power. And a revolution of the people is usually centered on a core theme or focus: to evenly redistribute power and the right of authority; the right to govern. But even if that is the intent… it rarely happens in full because over time human nature steps in, and that purpose unravels. A leadership faction forms within the masses and from that a strong personality begins to separate from weaker, though equally fervent believers and one person climbs to the top. They feel that to do so is their right. It is their individual manifest destiny to lead those that need to be directed.

How do they get there—to the top? A positive metaphor would be that they do so by creating stepping stones—that by looking at the landscape they identified and utilized natural support points—each one higher than the previous. Those are what they use to create (or follow) as a path to the summit. But that is not the way of the dictator. They (individually or as selectively established doctrine) take the fears of the masses—the crowd—that they harbor in their hearts and minds and use them to craft words to make them believe they can erase their fears. They are the solution to all their troubles and worries whether perceived or real.

And the misled masses form the foundation—the stages—from which the dictator rises. At the pinnacle, power consolidated and means of enforcement in place the words become rote propaganda that addresses, perhaps even smothers, the existence of those beneath the feet of the charismatic leader. The beliefs of the people and their hopes wane and disappear under the realization that all the blood, the trampling of individual rights, the replacement of free will and free thought with the dogma of the party... has not empowered the people. The suffering and sacrificing, even if only of their social conscience, was not worth what has materialized. Their realization is often too late to matter. What's done is done.

SINGAPORE—DECEMBER 1979

Jason Kenyon had filed that last article and returned to his hotel room. There he wondered for the thousandth time, what had happened to Scott Reynolds. Was he alive? He picked up the half full glass of whiskey and drank it off, the last swallow from the last bottle for him here in Singapore. He would be on a flight to the United States in three hours. It has been a long time, but he was going home. He got up from the small desk he had worked from since fleeing Vietnam in April of 1975. He knocked on the wood top with his knuckles. "If you're out there Scott, God bless you, and I hope you make it home one day, too." He picked up the single suitcase from the bed and stepped to the door. He reached over to turn out the lights then opened the door and left.

CHAPTER 41

Memorial Day 1998
Richard M. Nixon Library
Yorba Linda, California

The speakers were done and the audience rose to their feet. The talk of war and promises, both failed at so long ago, had raised painful memories in many and it showed on their faces as they stood.

As the crowd dispersed, he noticed that two people in the audience had remained in their chairs. Turning away, he wiped the tears from his face, pushed himself along with a cane, and began to move as quickly as he could. He heard steps behind him and realized the two women had left their seats and were walking fast, as if they suddenly couldn't get away quickly enough from the echoed speeches of moments ago. Soon they had caught up and were alongside him. When he realized it was them, he started to walk at an angle away. He could not let them see him and regretted that he had finally given in to what was eating him up inside—the desire to see his wife and daughter a final time.

The young woman was nearest to him. She brought a hand up to brush long, lustrous, black hair from her face. Her blue eyes, clearly Caucasian, complemented rather than contrasted the lighter olive tone, with just a hint of natural burnt umber, in her cheeks. He couldn't help it and stopped to look at her. The face of the older woman was a darker tint, but the high planes of their cheeks were the same. She removed her glasses to reposition them, and he saw that only the crinkling of lines around her eyes showed all the years that had passed. Suddenly, he smelled the scent of magnolia, and he remembered the texture of her skin as he touched it. He bowed his head and shuffled further out of their way. They had noticed him though and paused. He looked back at them over the rims of his sunglasses and met the eyes of the older woman, who was locked on him. The younger woman at her side looked at her and then at him.

He took a deep breath, removed his sunglasses, knowing that even a full beard did not hide what had become of his face. He straightened as much as his bent, and broken body would allow. He saw the tears coursing down the face of the older woman who had not flinched from him.

"We thought–" The older woman shook her head as if to clear it. "Why?"

Her tone raked him like nails drawing blood. He knew what she asked, and he owed her an answer; an explanation. "I had to see it through—the whole story—of what happened in Vietnam after the fall of Saigon." He looked at the younger woman who seemed as if she didn't know if she should cry or strike out at him. "And there was a young man and girl that needed help—I couldn't abandon them... and so many others that needed help. I have to tell their story, too." He turned to face the young woman who was now holding her mother and staring at him over her shoulder. "I'll explain... it's all tied together." The doubt in her eyes stabbed him. He felt them studying his face and he saw the pain in Mai's eyes and the tears welled, and she silently wept as she looked at him. "I know..." he touched his face, his fingers tracing the lines of the scars. "I could have come to you sooner... but... these." His fingers stopped moving and clenched into a fist in front of his face. "I'm so ugly now, Mai. How could I come to you, as a younger man looking like this and ruin everything you were doing to try and rebuild your life. A good one for your and Kim Phung." He looked at his daughter who was now crying, too. "So I stayed away until I couldn't bear it any longer. I needed to see you and to explain why the world needs to hear the next story I tell."

Mai came closer to him and her soft hands, the scent of her washed over him again, touched his ravaged face. She smoothed his hair, and her touch eased the pain that had been carved—permanently he thought—into his face. "I don't care about the story... since the day we met all I have cared about, other than our daughter, is you."

Scott raised his eyes and met hers. "I couldn't come home—like this—and ruin your chance to find happiness." He traced the scars on his face, his fingers coming away damp with the tears course down the channel of old wounds.

She took his hand from his face, leaned in closer, and he felt her lips kiss the scars. He closed his eyes and felt her lips on his. He opened them as he nuzzled her hair. The fragrance was one that he had endlessly dreamed of with each wind... hoping it would carry just a hint of it to him across the thousands of miles of ocean. Mai's arms were around him, pulling him tightly to her. He closed his eyes again. Then he felt another set of arms around him. Kim Phung's head was on his shoulder as she hugged him. He looked down at his beautiful daughter, so much like her mother at that age. She smiled up at him and smiled through the tears running down her cheeks.

"I love you, Daddy."

ABOUT THE AUTHOR

When South Vietnam was delivered to the evil North in April 1975, after many failed attempts Duyen Nguyen finally escaped and came to the U.S. in November 1984. Mr. Nguyen was one of the almost 800,000 refugees known as boat people, half of which settled in the United States. He now practices law in San Jose, California. With this novel Mr. Nguyen has written three books: The prequel to *When the Heart Cries but Never Breaks* is *Behind the Smoke Curtain*, a novel about Vietnam after the fall of Saigon in April 1975. He is also the author of the novel *CHIEF | The Story of a Pit Bull.*

A summary of both those stories accompanies on the following pages.

OTHER BOOKS BY THE AUTHOR

ABOUT BEHIND THE SMOKE CURTAIN

Mai was a beautiful young Vietnamese girl and a student at Saigon University. Scott was a young American reporter trying to establish himself as a freelance writer and journalist. Where better to seek that chance than in a war-torn country full of stories every day. They meet and fall in love just before the Tet offensive of 1968… when it became shockingly clear to the United States that the conflict in Vietnam was far from over. Caught up in the lies, intrigue, betrayals and violence of the war they suffer the impact of when Cold War opponents, behind their not so benign or altruistic curtain of diplomacy, pull the strings of a nation in turmoil. It is a sad and tragic truth that older men start the wars that the youth must fight and die in. Told as only a person who lived in Vietnam during that time knows it; this is the story of Mai and Scott as they try to live and love while their world disintegrates around them.

ABOUT *CHIEF* | *THE STORY OF A PIT BULL*

The story of a very brave dog that saved the life of a young wounded veteran and how she saved his. Both are scarred and damaged... but together—woman and dog— find love, trust, and peace. The very things they dreamed and wished for but thought they'd never have. Hannah is a combat wounded veteran; her face is disfigured, and she lost her left leg. Chief is a dog that escaped from a dogfighting ring that she adopted (against others advice because of his breed) as part of Wounded Warrior Project to help veterans. While traveling in Colorado, at a rest area, Hannah is attacked by a serial killer and rapist. Chief defends her. But the police take Chief from her (permissible under Denver/Colorado law) and plan to put him down. Hannah fights to save his life. Within this entertaining, sometimes heart-wrenching, tale, is a goal to raise empathy, compassion and awareness about animal cruelty... and how dogs that have experienced it can be saved and rehabilitated. And in turn, how they can be a benefit to a human... sometimes even saving them with their love.

www.ingramcontent.com/pod-product-compliance
Lightning Source LLC
Chambersburg PA
CBHW031945070426
42451CB00007BA/127